Southern Rails on the Isle of Wight
Volume Two:
The Ventnor and Bembridge Lines

Ian Drummond

With
Alan Doe

For
Andrew Drummond

Holne Publishing

© Holne Publishing, Ian Drummond & Alan Doe 2010

British Library Cataloguing in Publication Data
A record for this book is available from the British Library
ISBN 978-0-9563317-1-7
Published by: Holne Publishing, PO Box 343, LEEDS, LS19 9FW
Typeset by: Holne Publishing Services, PO Box 343, LEEDS, LS19 9FW
Printed by: Cambrian Printers, Aberystwyth

Reasonable efforts have been made to discover the true copyright owners of the photographs reproduced in this volume, and no infringement of copyright is intended. If you have any evidence about the copyright owner of any photograph, or the photographer of any photograph listed as 'photographer unknown', please contact the Publisher in the first instance. All uncredited photographs are by the author.

Photographs in this volume have been digitally adjusted to enhance clarity, and also remove blemishes, dust etc. However, no intentional alterations have been made to affect their historical significance.

Unless otherwise indicated for all maps North is at their top edge.

Holne Publishing
PO Box 343
LEEDS
LS19 9FW
enquiries@holnepublishing.co.uk
www.holnepublishing.co.uk

Cover Photos:
Front:
Top: W22 *Brading* steams into Ryde Esplanade station with a train for Cowes on 27th February 1965.
Bottom: W27 *Merstone* arrives at Sandown with a train for Ventnor on 27th February 1965.

Back: W35 *Freshwater* at Ventnor on 5th September 1964, in the background is the lorry belonging to W. Bates and Son Coal Merchants.

(All Photos David J. Mitchell)

Contents

W28 *Ashey* makes an impressive display as it departs from Brading in June 1965 with a train for Ventnor.
(Photo: A.J. Reeve Copyright Colour-Rail/BRS1572)

Foreword

With the frost showing white on the sleepers still in shade, W21 *Sandown* makes a fine sight departing from Ryde St John's Road with a train for Cowes on 27th February 1965. Note the drop-side goods wagon in the background.
(Photo: David J. Mitchell)

Many kind words have been said about Volume One of *Southern Rails on the Isle of Wight*, and it was particularly humbling to be jointly awarded the prize for Best Self-Published Book of 2010 by the David St John Thomas Charitable Trust. However, in a sense that applies extra pressure for this book.

I am though hopeful this volume will not disappoint. So many excellent photographs have come to light, most of which have not been published before, that it has been really difficult to decide what to leave out. In the end it was easier to add some pages rather than miss out on the wealth of material available. Sadly, however, lack of space has still precluded covering the Southern Railway's involvement with the Southern Vectis Bus Company, and also air services.

It is also good that Alan Doe, who has conducted extensive research on The Bembridge branch, has contributed much of the material for that section of the book for which I am grateful. My thanks must again go to the staff and volunteers at the Isle of Wight Steam Railway and its archives, particularly

Roger Silsbury, Terry Hastings, Paddy Jardine and Norman Therle for all their help. My gratitude goes too to the staff at the National Railway Museum, The Isle of Wight Record Office and *Stagecoach*, who have all provided much assistance.

My wife, Di, has once more been so encouraging and supportive to this project. Thanks too to Lawrie Bowles, and Barbara Varley for their help in proof-reading the manuscript, as well as to many others too numerous to mention, for all their encouragement.

There is such a rich body of information to draw upon about the history of the Island's railways, and so I am grateful to the authors of all the books mentioned in the bibliography for their work. The contribution of all the photographers whose work is featured in this volume also has to be noted, for without them this book would be much the poorer.

Finally this book is dedicated to the memory of my eldest brother, Andrew, who saw my first book published, but sadly did not see this one.

Map of the Isle of Wight Railways

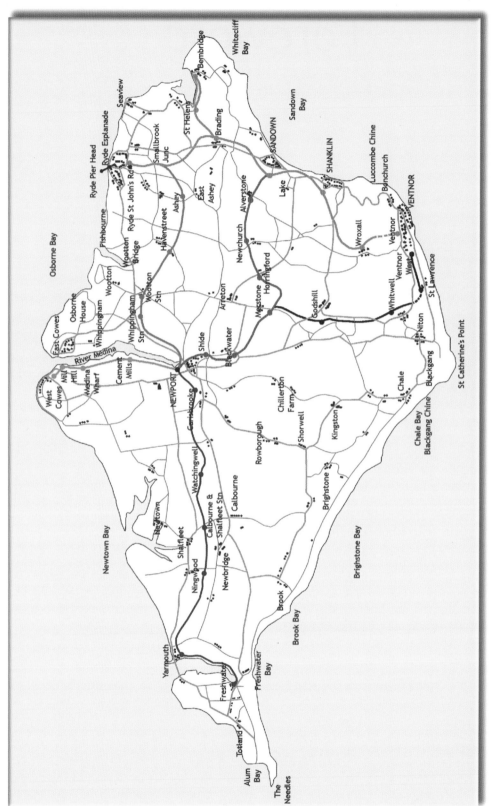

KEY:

——— Cowes & Newport Railway (C&NR)

——— Isle of Wight Railway (IWR)

——— Ryde & Newport Railway (R&NR)

——— Isle of Wight (Newport Junction) Railway (IW(NJ)R)

——— Freshwater, Yarmouth & Newport Railway (FYNR)

——— Newport, Godshill & St Lawrence Railway (NG&SLR)

The Isle of Wight Railway

A preserved panel from ex-IWR coach No.19

Introduction

The relative success of the Isle of Wight Railway (IWR), compared with the other lines on the Island, probably owes itself to a number of factors. First among these are those which relate to geography, in that the IWR served the resorts on the leeward side of the Island that were sheltered from the prevailing westerly winds, and had lovely sandy beaches.

Another contribution from its geography was the relatively short sea crossing between Ryde and Portsmouth. This was a crossing which, in the latter years of the nineteenth century, both the London & South Western Railway (LSWR) and the London, Brighton & South Coast Railway (LBSCR) were keen to develop. They were even prepared to invest in the Island's railway infrastructure.

Royalty was the next factor, with Queen Victoria and Prince Albert making Osborne House their summer residence. This made the Island the place to visit for the fashionable holiday-maker in the mid-nineteenth century.

Finally there was the involvement as a Company Director of Captain Mark Huish, former chairman of the London and North Western Railway (LNWR), who was retired and living at Bonchurch. He brought much needed railway operating experience to the enterprise. However, despite all these advantages it was a close run thing that the railway was both built and survived to become the Isle of Wight's 'Premier Line'.

Origins

A number of schemes for public railways were proposed on the Island in the mid-nineteenth century including some between Ryde and Ventnor. What was to become the IWR was originally known as the Isle of Wight (Eastern Section) Railway (IW(ES)R). It had, in 1858, proposed a line from Ryde to Bonchurch running east of Brading to Sandown and Shanklin before heading south to its destination via Luccombe, but its Bill was thrown out by Parliament.

However, in 1860 another Bill was submitted for a line from Ryde to Ventnor. At Ryde the line was to start at Melville Street, and proceed via Brading, Sandown and Shanklin before now turning inland to Wroxall. It would then go south towards Ventnor passing through a tunnel under the Downs and terminate in a quarry high above the town. There was also a proposed tramway to the pier at Ryde, a branch to Brading Quay, a branch to Sandown Bay, and a line to run from Smallbrook to Newport and connect with the Cowes and Newport Railway (C&NR). In the event only the line between Ryde and Ventnor, and the branch to Brading Quay were built.

Left: An early picture showing the original station building at Ryde St John's Road.
(Photo: IWSR Collection)

Initially there were eleven return trips between Ryde and Shanklin, where coaches met some of the trains for connections to and from Ventnor. There were also two trains on Sunday. However, connections with the ferries to and from either Portsmouth or Stokes Bay could be described as 'variable', demonstrating a distinct lack of co-ordination. Despite this, passenger numbers exceeded expectations.

Construction

The Act incorporating the IW(ES)R became law on 23rd July 1860, and Henry Bond was awarded the construction contract in December 1862, when, with little ceremony, work commenced. Another experienced railwayman, John Fowler, was appointed as engineer, and in February 1863 he was able to report that work on the Ventnor tunnel had started. However, it was not long before water ingress was to bedevil the work. A powerful pump had to be imported to keep construction going.

As usual the optimism that the work would be speedily completed proved unfounded, and it would not be until August 1864 that the line between Ryde and Shanklin was ready for inspection. Happily it was passed at the first attempt, and services started on 23rd August.

Opening and Operating

At Ryde the decision had been made to make St John's Road the temporary terminus of the line and a wooden station, along with locomotive and carriage facilities, was built there. It was here at 6am that about a dozen passengers gathered in the pouring rain on opening day to take the first train. After this somewhat subdued start things improved and about 4,000 people rode the trains during the first four days of operation.

Meanwhile work on the extension to Ventnor continued and by August 1864 there was a complete bore through the Downs. Finally the line was opened for traffic on 10th September 1866, but by then the IWR was in financial difficulties. Nevertheless, the usual celebrations were organised for the event, including a fireworks display.

By the summer of 1867 the train service consisted of fourteen return trains on weekdays. However, Captain Huish's contribution to the IWR had come to an abrupt end with his death in January 1867.

Expansion Plans

As the IW(ES)R's name implied, the Ryde-Ventnor line was seen as simply the first of a network of lines that would traverse the Island. Therefore, even while the original line was being built, plans were already in hand for extensions with lines from Smallbrook to Newport, with a link to the C&NR, and then south to Wroxall. This was authorised in 1863, but without the connection to the C&NR. The Bill also empowered the Company to change its name to The Isle of Wight Railway Company (IWR).

However, the expenditure involved in promoting these schemes, along with escalating construction costs, merely served to increase the Company's financial difficulties. Finally, in 1868, the Company abandoned all expansion plans.

Consolidation and Other Lines

The financial crisis continued despite healthy passenger numbers, with some 394,000 being carried in 1869, and an operating profit of around £7,000. Gradually, though, with increasing traffic the financial situation eased.

In the 1870s two new railways connected with the IWR, the first to begin operation was the Isle of Wight (Newport Junction) Railway (IW(NJ)R), which opened between Sandown and Shide in February 1875, and to Newport in June 1879. This line was initially operated in conjunction with the IWR, but later came under the Joint Committee with the C&NR and the Ryde and Newport Railway (R&NR). The latter was opened between Ryde St John's Road and Newport in December 1875, with a new line being laid alongside the IWR line between Smallbrook and St John's Road.

It was at this time that a solution was found to the issue of connecting the station at Ryde St John's Road with the ferries at Ryde Pier. There had been negotiations with the Ryde Commissioners for some time to extend the line north to Melville Street and on to the pier, but without success. In the event the Ryde Pier Company obtained an Act to extend its tramway from the pier to St John's Road, which opened in 1871, but this did not prove a satisfactory long-term solution (see the section on the Ryde Pier Tramway).

However, the LSWR and the LBSCR were looking to develop the cross-Solent traffic travelling between Portsmouth and Ryde, and so were willing to build the line including building a third pier to carry the railway out to the pier head. They were then prepared, after a little persuasion, to allow the IWR and R&NR to operate their trains on it, in return for a suitable proportion of the receipts of course.

This line opened for the operation of IWR trains to Ryde Esplanade on 5th April 1880, and to Ryde Pier Head on 12th July. By this time the mainland companies had also taken over the ferry operations, and so the most straightforward connection between ferry and rail on the Island was established. R&NR trains began to work through from 4th October 1880.

Another new line to connect with the IWR was the line to St Helens and Bembridge, which fully opened on 27th May 1882. This connected with the IWR at Brading, and was purchased by them in 1898.

1887 saw the establishment of the Isle of Wight Central Railway (IWCR) incorporating the C&NR, R&NR and IW(NJ)R. This the IWR viewed with suspicion, and opposed the Bill establishing the IWCR in Parliament, as it feared the new entity would close the R&NR. Therefore, it insisted on a clause specifying a minimum level of services on the line being inserted in the Act.

Above: An early view at Ventnor with two bolster wagons and a consignment of timber. The narrow entrance to the tunnel and lack of signal box can be compared to later photos elsewhere in this book.   (Photo: IWSR Collection)

Further Progress

Other developments followed as passenger numbers increased. In fact such was the pressure of passenger operations that goods trains had to be operated at night.

A halt was opened to serve the County Cricket Ground at Lake in 1889. In response to new legislation, Webb & Thompson Electric Train Staff equipment was installed on the line in 1891, while Westinghouse air brakes were fitted to locomotives and stock the following year.

By the turn of the century there was a second station at Ventnor Town, the Newport, Godshill and St Lawrence Railway (NG&SLR) having opened throughout in 1900. However, the new line did not diminish the growth in traffic on the IWR.

There had though been several proposals for making the line more accessible at Ventnor. First were plans for a network of tramways, and then in 1889 the idea of a funicular railway between the Esplanade Hotel and the station, even possibly extending to the top of St Boniface Down, was developed. Sadly the scheme never came to fruition, but the concept was revived on a number of occasions, and even the Southern Railway (SR) considered the option seriously. The idea was only finally abandoned in 1927.

World War One

The early years of the twentieth century saw more improvements to stations and trains as passenger numbers increased. In 1913 the IWR carried over one million passengers, while 1914 saw the introduction of third class fares on all trains, except for through tickets to the mainland. But the advent of World War One brought a rapid decline in the tourist trade with Ventnor being particularly badly hit.

Like other railways, the IWR benefited from the government's compensation scheme, which reimbursed the Company for loss of takings due to the war up to the level of their 1913 income. However, capital expenditure was restricted, with the result that by the end of the war its infrastructure had deteriorated significantly.

War had brought other changes. The railway employed its first woman in 1917 as a 'girl messenger', and even had a stationmistress at Wroxall for a short time. Following the war traffic began to increase again, but there was still insufficient income to fund the major improvements required for the line. By now too, events elsewhere were to lead to the end of the independent life of the IWR, when it became part of the Southern Railway in 1923.

Left: W15 *Cowes* at Shanklin with a train for Ventnor on 27th June 1939.
(Photo: H.W. Robinson Copyright J.F. Hyde Steam Archive)

The Southern Railway

As with the lines of the former IWCR and FYNR, one of the first priorities of the Southern was to strengthen the permanent way on the ex-IWR's lines, in order to make use of the ex-LSWR Adams O2 class locomotives now being imported to the Island. However, as the IWR's civil engineering structures were more robust than those of the other lines this did not take as long to complete.

Signals were also renewed with ex-LSWR fittings on lattice posts. New fixtures were installed, such as nameboards, and by the mid 1930s the line was said to be up to the standard of the mainland.

A crossing loop at Wroxall was to be the first major improvement on the line. This came into use in July 1924, and featured the installation of Electric Staff instruments in the booking office.

Extra capacity was desperately needed as, with the popularity of Island holidays, passenger numbers were increasing rapidly. Therefore, 1926 saw the start of a major re-construction of the station buildings at Ryde Pier Head. The same year saw a crossover and new signal box erected at Smallbrook, so that the line from there to St John's Road could be operated as double-track in the summer, reverting to single-track working in winter. At the same time approval was given for the doubling of the line from Brading to Sandown, which was completed in June 1927 at a cost of £28,000 (approx. £1.4million today).

This allowed three trains per hour to depart from Ryde Pier Head for the Ventnor line on Saturdays in 1930. With the addition of a fourth platform at Pier Head in 1933 this increased to four, one being a short working to Sandown, with a fifth for the Cowes line. By this time too the Southern had begun to encourage the use of Passenger Luggage in Advance (PLA) to ease accommodation problems on ordinary trains. In 1935 there were two return

W34 *Newport* arrived on the Island in May 1947 painted in LSWR Green, it was repainted malachite on the tank sides and bunker and re-lettered *British Railways*, and is seen in this 'hybrid' livery in May 1952.
(Photo: S.C. Townroe Copyright Colour-Rail/BRS829)

workings on Fridays with additional capacity on Thursdays specifically for this traffic. There was also a daily fish and parcels train.

In addition there were through trains introduced in 1930 which ran between Newport and Shanklin, and from Cowes to Ventnor. There were then the *East-West Through Trains* introduced between Shanklin (Sandown on Saturdays) and Freshwater in 1932. These were renamed *The Tourist* in 1933 and ran as a semi-fast Monday to Saturday between Ventnor and Freshwater.

Throughout this period there were continuing improvements to all the stations, as well as to the locomotive and workshop facilities at Ryde St John's Road, but still there seemed no end to the increasing traffic. In the late 1930s options were considered for improving the service further including doubling the whole line, or providing extra facilities on the existing line to permit six trains an hour to depart from Ryde Pier Head. However, the coming of the Second World War put paid to these plans.

World War Two

On 11th September 1939 the service on the Ryde-Ventnor line was reduced to six trains a day, such was the impact of the outbreak of hostilities. Travel restrictions were imposed, and Ryde Pier apparently only just escaped being blown up by an over-enthusiastic army officer to prevent it being used in an invasion.

There were several attacks which affected the line during the war. Among the most serious was an explosion which damaged the track on 12th August 1940 at Three-arch bridge between Shanklin and Wroxall. Later that year, on 5th December, a bomb fell just north of Ryde St John's Road, derailing the locomotive of a Ventnor-bound train, but with no casualties.

The line also played a part in the D-day preparations with the 'Operation Pluto' pipeline being laid alongside the line between Smallbrook and Sandown in 1944. This supplied fuel to the Normandy landing sites, and played a vital role in the success of the operation.

Nationalisation

Even before the war was formally concluded plans were already being made for the post-war resumption of services. In August 1944 clearance checks were made in preparation for the import of more powerful locomotives for a push-pull service operating with six-coach trains on the line. Much work was done for the arrival of E4 class 0-6-2T No.2510 in February 1947, but in the end the scheme proved abortive.

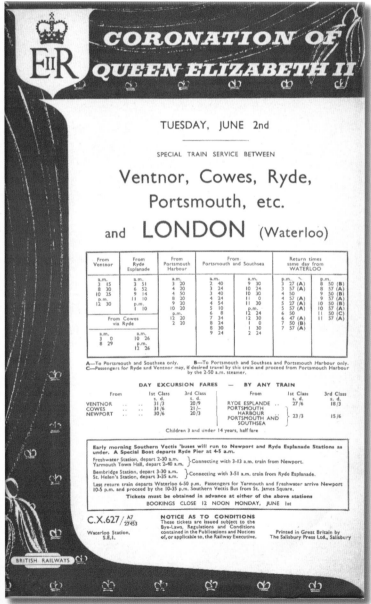

Meanwhile in 1945 the Ryde-Ventnor line resumed a half-hourly service, with three trains an hour on summer Saturdays when required. Even *The Tourist* through trains ran again. 1946 saw further improvements, but in 1947 services were restricted due to a national coal shortage. By now though, the line was destined to become part of British Railways (BR) on 1st January 1948.

As was seen in Volume One, the closure of all the Island lines was discussed in the early 1950s. In fact in one scheme only the line between Ryde Pier Head and Ryde St John's Road would be retained. During the 1950s the large summer traffic remained, but was showing signs of decline, the 4.4 million passengers who had used the Portsmouth-Ryde ferry in 1953 becoming 3.4 million by 1961. At the same time the number of cars using the Portsmouth-Fishbourne Ferry increased from 26,677 to 74,081, there was a sea-change happening in the tourist trade.

Closure of the Bembridge branch in 1953, and the line between Sandown and Newport in 1956 also had an impact. The latter bringing to an end the through trains to Cowes and Newport that had run from Ventnor.

In 1963 what became known as *The Beeching Report* advocated the closure of all the remaining lines on the Island. After huge local opposition it was decided to close all but the Ryde-Shanklin line, and BR announced its intention to end trains on the Shanklin-Ventnor and Ryde-Cowes lines from 4th October 1965. However, after many objections, a stay of execution was granted, but in the end the Cowes line closed from 21st February 1966. The last trains ran on the Ventnor section on Sunday 17th April 1966, with large crowds there to ride or see the final trains.

Meanwhile the line between Ryde and Shanklin was also closed, but in this case to allow it to be converted to electric operation. Therefore, the final passenger steam trains on the Island to be operated by BR ran on the last day of 1966 with hundreds of people witnessing the event. However, as we will see, it was not the end either for the Ryde-Shanklin line, or for steam on the Island, as both were destined to return.

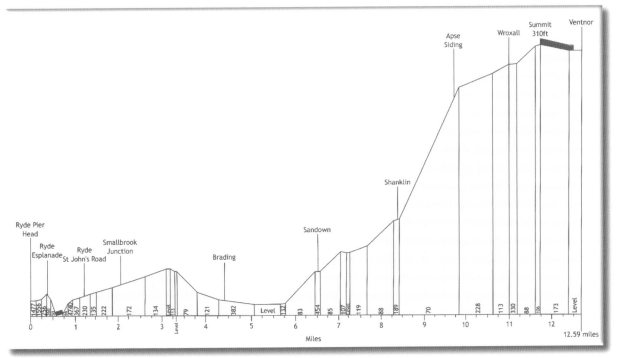

Gradient Map of the line from Ryde Pier Head to Ventnor
Based on a Gradient Map from the IWSR Archive
(Gradients in form 1 in x and distances from Ryde Pier Head)

Map of Ryde to Ventnor Line
Based on Ordnance Survey Map of 1919

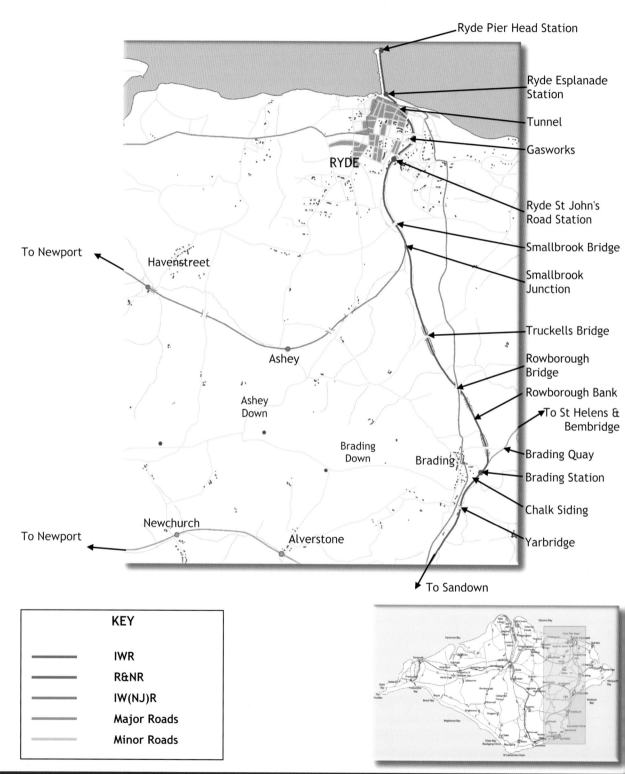

Ryde Pier Head Station

Ryde Esplanade Station

Tunnel

Gasworks

RYDE

Ryde St John's Road Station

Smallbrook Bridge

To Newport

Havenstreet

Smallbrook Junction

Truckells Bridge

Rowborough Bridge

Ashey

Rowborough Bank

Ashey Down

To St Helens & Bembridge

Brading Down

Brading

Brading Quay

Brading Station

Chalk Siding

Newchurch

To Newport

Alverstone

Yarbridge

To Sandown

KEY

———	IWR
———	R&NR
———	IW(NJ)R
———	Major Roads
———	Minor Roads

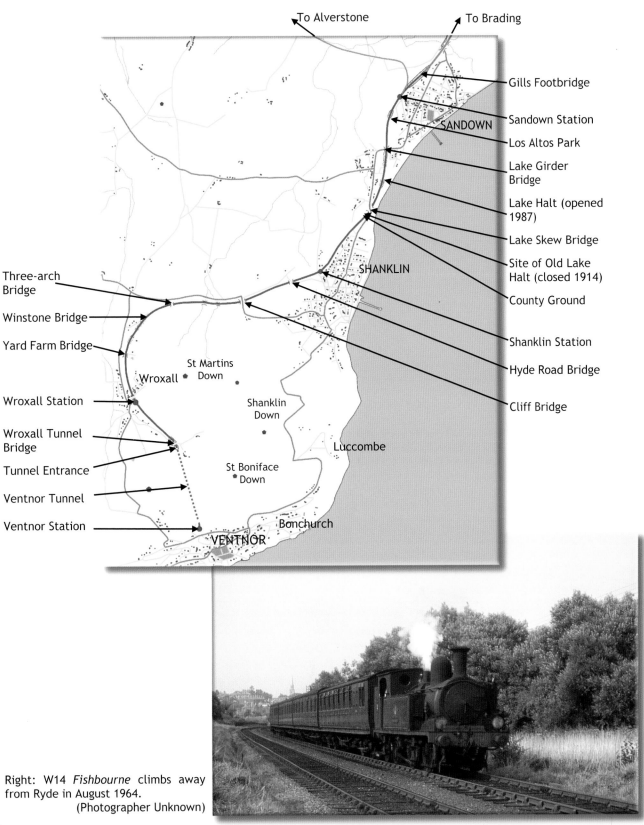

To Alverstone

To Brading

Gills Footbridge

Sandown Station

SANDOWN

Los Altos Park

Lake Girder Bridge

Lake Halt (opened 1987)

Lake Skew Bridge

Site of Old Lake Halt (closed 1914)

County Ground

SHANKLIN

Shanklin Station

Hyde Road Bridge

Three-arch Bridge

Winstone Bridge

Yard Farm Bridge

Cliff Bridge

St Martins Down

Wroxall

Shanklin Down

Wroxall Station

Luccombe

Wroxall Tunnel Bridge

St Boniface Down

Tunnel Entrance

Ventnor Tunnel

Ventnor Station

Bonchurch

VENTNOR

Right: W14 *Fishbourne* climbs away from Ryde in August 1964.
(Photographer Unknown)

Ryde Pier Head

W24 *Calbourne* chases the seagulls as it departs with the Cowes-bound *Vectis Farewell* Locomotive Club of Great Britain railtour on 3rd October 1965. This was organised in anticipation of the closure of the Ryde-Cowes line the next day, but in the event the line did not close until the following year. (Photo: David J. Mitchell)

Of course chronologically the first station in Ryde was at St John's Road, Pier Head only coming into operation following the full opening of the Joint Line to IWR trains on 12th July 1880, and to R&NR trains on 4th October the same year. However, it was to become the place where hundreds of thousands of people had their first encounter with the Island, and its railway system, often waiting in long queues for a train.

The line from Ryde Esplanade to Ryde Pier Head was built along a third pier, parallel to the original promenade and tramway piers, being the easternmost of the three. It is nearly a half a mile long stretching out into the Solent to meet the ferries plying to and from Portsmouth.

Pier Head station was constructed with wooden station buildings at the end of the three 400ft platform roads at right angles to the line. There were two platforms, one on the western side serving road number one, while the second was an island platform between roads two and three.

Between the platforms there was a crossover connecting roads one and two to permit locomotives to run round their train. At first there were no watering or coaling facilities at Pier Head, locomotives having to return to St John's Road for servicing.

Trains normally arrived at platform one and, once the locomotive had run round, were moved to one of the other platforms ready for departure. However, the signalling allowed for trains to arrive and depart from any platform. Beyond the end of the platforms was a wooden signal box supplied with a 28-lever frame in front of which was a scissors crossover. The LSWR, who with the LBSCR owned the line to St John's Road until Grouping, replaced much of the signalling in 1907.

In 1892 equipment was installed at the station for the 'heating of foot-warmers'. These were supplied to passengers at an additional cost until the arrival of steam heated stock, which doubtless made a considerable difference in winter.

Left: Around 1900 IWR locomotive *Brading* waits at Pier Head with a Ventnor train composed of IWR four-wheel stock.
(Photographer Unknown)

Below: A postcard from around the same period shows the three piers. A train departs from the station on the left, in the centre the tramway can be seen with the promenade pier on the right.
(IWSR Collection)

Until the completion of the new facilities at Medina Wharf, Pier Head station was used for the loading and unloading of locomotives, as well as other items travelling to and from the Island. Thus in 1916 the IWR's locomotive *Bembridge* departed by this route, for service with the War Department. In the other direction the first O2 class locomotives arrived there in 1923.

When the Southern took over the station in 1923 returns indicate that some 15,553 tickets were issued in the busiest month, and 10,815 collected. However this would not include transit passengers with tickets to and from the mainland connecting with other stations on the Island. On Whit Monday 1924 alone 19,000 passengers are said to have passed through the station. This put a heavy load on the station facilities.

Above: The original station building at Pier Head in 1920. (Photo: IWSR Collection)

Therefore, it was not long before the station buildings were replaced, being completed in 1926. The new construction comprised of steel framing with brick and roughcast facing. Three of the four steam cranes on the pier head were also replaced with electric ones. A glazed roof, and weather screen on the west side of the station were supplied as well as 'improved locomotive watering facilities', probably being the water tower.

Further developments came with the addition of a fourth platform road, this was built on the western side of platform one. Other work included the renewal of the existing platforms in concrete, surfacing them with asphalt, and providing new canopies. When this was completed in 1933 the platforms were re-numbered from east to west. All this allowed up to five trains an hour to depart on summer Saturdays in the late 1930s.

Ryde Pier suffered little bomb damage during the Second World War, but did come under fire, being strafed by enemy aircraft on at least one occasion. In the summer of 1945 two trains an hour were again departing from the station for Ventnor, increasing to three in 1949, by then of course ownership of the station had changed with British Railways taking charge in 1948.

The 1950s brought increased numbers of holiday makers to the Island. Special trains operated for Queen Elizabeth's 'Review of the Fleet' on 15th June 1953, just as they had done for Queen Victoria's jubilees, when grandstands were built on the pier head.

During the winter of 1958-59 the permanent way through Ryde Esplanade, along the pier and throughout Pier Head station was renewed. Additional awnings were also provided for those waiting for ferries.

In 1963, despite uncertainty over the long-term future of the line, authorisation was given for the rebuilding of the railway pier. Traffic was still heavy and on 10th August 1963 54,507 passengers passed through the station.

British Rail passenger steam trains finally ended on 31st December 1966, but Pier Head station had already seen its last steam passenger train on 17th September 1966, as it had been closed to permit the start of the changes for electrification. These will be dealt with later in this book. However, by now the heyday of the station had passed, and never would the crowds of earlier days be seen there again.

Above: W19, later named *Osborne*, at Pier Head on 20th June 1928 with a train of ex-London, Chatham and Dover Railway four-wheelers.   (Photo: F.J. Agar Copyright P.J. Fidczuk)

Below: W23 *Totland* receives a check-over on Ryde Pier on 4th August 1931.
                                                                         (Photo: L. Hanson Copyright D. Hanson)

Above: W35 *Freshwater* prepares to depart from platform two with a short Ventnor train on 9th April 1966, the last week the line between Shanklin and Ventnor would be open. (Photo: P.F. Bloxam)

Below: W30 *Shorwell* running round its train at Pier Head on 27th February 1965. Note the weathering effects on the carriage ends. (Photo: David J. Mitchell)

Above: W27 *Merstone* approaches platform four at Pier Head on 27th February 1965. Note the water tower provided by the Southern Railway in the 1920s between platforms one and two, and the bell mounted on the post just behind W27. This was rung to warn train crews of an approaching ferry. The terminus of the tramway can also be seen on the left.

Below: A grubby W24 *Calbourne* eases out of the station with a Ventnor train on 5th September 1964. A ferry is tied up at the berth behind.

(Both Photos: David J. Mitchell)

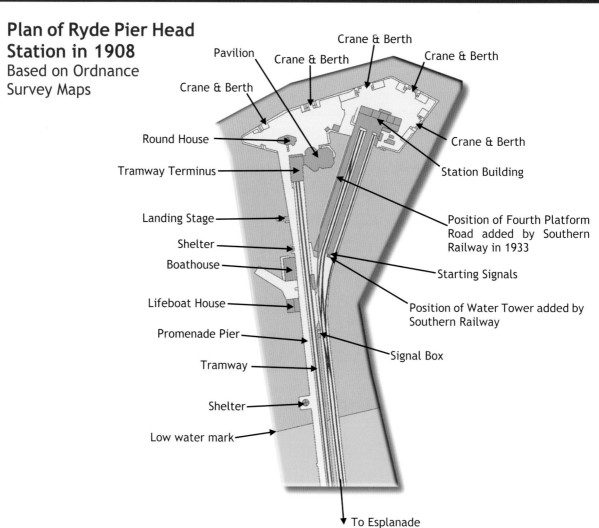

Plan of Ryde Pier Head Station in 1908
Based on Ordnance Survey Maps

Pavilion

Crane & Berth

Crane & Berth

Crane & Berth

Crane & Berth

Crane & Berth

Round House

Tramway Terminus

Station Building

Landing Stage

Position of Fourth Platform Road added by Southern Railway in 1933

Shelter

Boathouse

Starting Signals

Lifeboat House

Position of Water Tower added by Southern Railway

Promenade Pier

Tramway

Signal Box

Shelter

Low water mark

To Esplanade

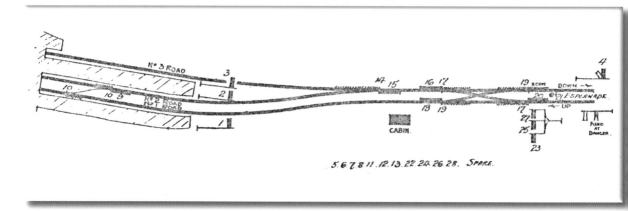

Signalling Plan of Ryde Pier Head in 1924

Ryde Esplanade

Above: A classic picture. W16 *Ventnor* stands at Ryde Esplanade with a train for Cowes on 18th December 1962. In the background a tramcar can be seen in the tram terminus. (Photo: David J. Mitchell)

From Ryde Pier Head a train would travel down the half mile length of the pier before encountering a sharp left hand curve of nine chains radius and enter Ryde Esplanade station. Esplanade was opened to IWR trains on 5th April 1880, just a few months before the Pier Head station, and, like Pier Head, to R&NR trains on 4th October.

It was built beside the tramway station, and consisted of two wooden platforms built on the curve (no sidings being constructed due to opposition from the Ryde Corporation) with the Down, or easternmost, platform built out over the sea. They were connected by means of a subway. On the Down platform there was a waiting shelter, small staff room, weather screen and canopy, while the on the Up side there was a booking office, waiting room, and canopy.

At the southern end of the Up platform stood a 12-lever signal box, which existed until July 1922,

when it was closed and control was passed to the box at Pier Head. At that point the base of the box, which contained a large gas meter, was retained and covered over. Initially the mainland companies rented some offices from the Pier Company, but following a dispute in 1887 they constructed wooden buildings to provide a parcels office and toilets. In 1906 more buildings were added in the shape of a new waiting room and extended parcels accommodation.

SOUTHERN RAILWAY.

RYDE ESPLANADE

On 22nd May 1899 either IWCR No.1 or No.2 enters Ryde Esplanade station with a train from Newport. Note the check rail on the curve and also the LBSCR pattern signal. (Photo: LCGB/Ken Nunn Collection)

The pier was damaged on several occasions. One such occurrence was caused by gales in 1916, and resulted in damage to 220ft of the Down platform.

In terms of passenger bookings Esplanade was by far the busiest of the three Ryde stations, with 32,390 tickets issued during the heaviest month of 1923, and some 87,000 tickets collected. Annual passenger receipts for that year amounted to £22,310 15s 7½d (£22,310.78).

Following Grouping the Southern decided to replace many of the timber buildings at Esplanade with new brick built structures. These included ticket, parcels and enquiry offices, as well as toilets. They were in use in 1930, and in this form the station continued, except for maintenance of the station and permanent way, until electrification.

With the temporary closure of Ryde Pier Head for electrification work in September 1966, Esplanade became the terminus for the line. The Down line was also out of use, and so trains were worked to the station being 'topped and tailed' by two locomotives from St John's Road to remove the need for a run-round.

It was therefore at Esplanade that the last steam passenger train for Shanklin departed at 9.53pm on 31st December 1966 with W14 *Fishbourne* in charge, and driver Peter Harbour at the regulator assisted by fireman Ray Knapp. At the rear was W27 *Merstone*, which had pulled the last train on the first Island line to close, from Ventnor West to Merstone in 1952. Hundreds of people gathered on the platforms, as well as crowding onto the train, to witness the end of an era.

However, for Ryde Esplanade the story continues as *Island Line* trains still call at its Up platform on their way to and from Pier Head. There had been plans for a major interchange to be built here, but these seem to have been abandoned. However, it is likely that Esplanade will continue to play its part in the railway history of the Island for many years to come.

Above: There is much to see in this turn of the century view. The signal box is clearly visible, and just to its right the station nameboard. Below the nameboard the sign reads *For trains to all stations on the Isle of Wight and to stations on the London and South Western and London, Brighton and South Coast Railways.* On the right a barge is being towed with a cargo for the mainland. Meanwhile an IWR 2-4-0T locomotive pauses in the station with a train for Ventnor. (Photo: IWSR Collection)

Left: Esplanade station in February 2010 is a shadow of what it once was with only a single line in use along the pier. The original buildings and canopy on the Down platform were demolished in 1978 to be replaced with a waiting shelter, while the rusting rails on the right tell their own story.

Above: W23, later named *Totland*, pauses at Ryde Esplanade with a train for Ventnor on 20th June 1928.
(Photo: F.J. Agar Copyright P.J. Fidczuk)

Below: W27 *Merstone* is nearly at the end of its journey as it prepares to depart from Ryde Esplanade for Pier Head on 27th February 1965. Judging by the oxy-acetylene cylinders on the left some work is being done.
(Photo: David J. Mitchell)

Ryde Esplanade Station in 1939
Based on Ordnance Survey Maps

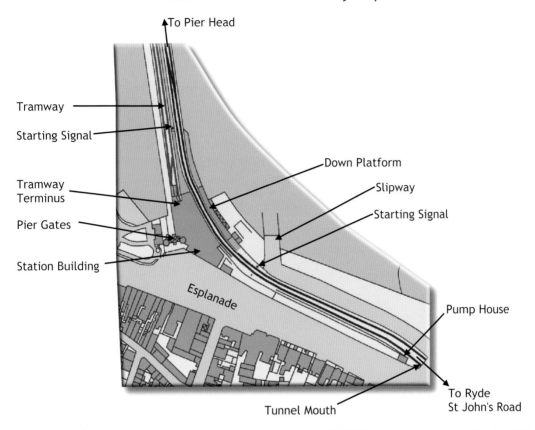

To Pier Head

Tramway

Starting Signal

Tramway Terminus

Pier Gates

Station Building

Down Platform

Slipway

Starting Signal

Esplanade

Pump House

Tunnel Mouth

To Ryde St John's Road

Right: At the end of steam operations W28 *Ashey* is exuding steam from every orifice as it departs from Ryde Esplanade.
(Photographer Unknown)

Above: On 27th February 1965 W14 *Fishbourne* departs down the grade for Ryde St John's Road with a Ventnor line train, while just behind the bus a train can be seen moving towards Pier Head, and on the left is the pump house.
(Photo: David J. Mitchell)

Below: The southern portal of Esplanade Tunnel, with W35 *Freshwater* on 5th September 1964. Note the concrete buttressing added to prevent movement of the retaining wall.
(Photo: David J. Mitchell)

Through the Years in Ryde

Right: At the beginning of the 20th Century an IWR Beyer-Peacock with a train of IWR four-wheelers storms up the line from Esplanade towards Rink Road overbridge.
(Commercial Postcard)

Above: On the last day of steam working, with the line to Pier Head closed and the conductor rail for the electric trains laid, trains were 'topped and tailed' with locomotives for working between Ryde St John's Road and Esplanade and reverse. Here W18 *Ningwood* with an unidentified O2 in the rear climbs from the tunnel under Rink Road bridge for one of the last times on 31st December 1966. (Photo: P.F. Bloxam)

Right: The scene from Rink Road overbridge in February 2010.

Left: After going under Rink Road overbridge trains now passed Ryde gasworks. Here there was a network of sidings until the gasworks closed and the sidings were clipped out of use in May 1958. W21 *Sandown* passes the works on 7th July 1957 with a Ventnor train.
(Photo: Nick Nicolson Copyright transporttreasury.co.uk)

Right: A similar view from the Park Road overbridge in February 2010.

Left: Having passed under the Park Road overbridge trains rounded the curve onto the northern throat of St John's Road. Here W33 *Bembridge* passes the Down Home signal for St John's Road on 7th August 1965.
(Photo: Courtesy Ernie Brack)

Ryde St John's Road

Above: W29 *Alverstone* approaches Ryde St John's Road with the 12.25pm train from Ryde Pier Head for Ventnor on 16th October 1965. The P.W. Store on the right was formed from the base of the old North signal box.

(Photo: P.F. Bloxam)

Ryde Esplanade station is on a downward grade, which increases to I in 50 as a train departs from the station, and drops towards the 391yds long Esplanade Tunnel. This section is actually built on the remains of the tidal basin developed by the Isle of Wight Ferry Company (see page 156).

The tunnel was constructed by a cut and cover method, and is actually a single bore, although the tunnel entrances would cause you to think otherwise. In the deepest section the roof was supported on wrought iron girders. As the tunnel-floor is below sea-level it was subject to regular water ingress. Therefore, a pump house was provided at the Esplanade entrance beside the Up line. Even so the tunnel was still regularly flooded during adverse weather, with consequent disruption of services.

Moving through the tunnel the gradient changes to an upward grade of 1 in 66, and the train emerges from the south portal more or less at the site of the intended terminus of the IW(ES)R at Melville Street. Movements in the retaining wall here in 1915 led to the installation of concrete struts under the track supporting a new concrete wall.

From here the line follows the route of the old tramway alongside Monkton Mead Brook. Passing under Rink Road bridge Ryde gasworks was reached on the western side of the track. Here a series of private sidings sprang from a turnout in the Up line, and was the northern limit of regular goods working on the line. The siding was closed on 23rd May 1958.

Park Road bridge is the next landmark reached, before the line passes the site of the tramway carriage shed. This is followed by the remains of St John's Road North signal box, then under St John's

Above: W27 *Merstone* starts away from St John's Road in July 1965. (Photographer Unknown)

Road bridge, which marked the division between the Joint Line and the IWR, and into the station itself.

St John's Road was established by the IWR as its 'temporary' northern terminus in 1864. It was originally provided with a wooden building and platform with a run-round loop. To the west of this a goods shed with its own run-round loop was situated, while to the east of the line a 156ft long three-road wooden carriage shed, and 72ft two-road brick-built engine shed were built (see plan on page 38).

It was not long before further facilities were necessary, so a second platform was added on the opposite side of the run-round loop. In addition the station building was extended to provide extra accommodation.

1868 saw the construction of a wagon repair shop, and subsequent years saw further workshop developments including a new stone-built locomotive erecting shop and smithy. Further

equipment came in the form of a traverser in 1870 along with a new water tank and windmill to pump water from a well. A new corrugated-iron locomotive running shed was built to the west of the main line in 1873 with a coal stage, although, due to a land dispute, the IWR was unable to make use of it until 1874. Meanwhile, the old shed was converted into a machine shop. Another corrugated-iron carriage and wagon shop was erected south of the existing workshops in 1876 (see plan on page 38).

By this point other developments had taken place at St John's Road. First was the arrival of the Pier Tramway in 1871 (see page 156). A new wooden island platform was constructed on the Down side of the IWR line, and the two IWR roads were extended across St John's Road on a level crossing with the tramway. This meant that in order to run round its train a locomotive had to cross the road, something which was technically illegal. The main platform was also extended with the removal of the run-round loop to the goods shed.

Left: In the early days of the Southern Railway W14 *Shanklin* stands outside the old engine shed at St John's Road.
(Photographer Unknown)

Below: The Southern Railway built a new engine shed which came into use in May 1930. Shortly after this *Terrier* W12 *Ventnor*, and either *Ryde* or *Wroxall* can be seen behind. Beyond the engine shed is the coal stage.
(Photo: IWSR Collection)

However, more change was to come with the arrival of the R&NR in 1875. This approached the station on a separate line to the west of the IWR from Smallbrook. It was not the R&NR's original intention to terminate at St John's Road. They had authority for their trains to go as far as Simeon Street on a line laid beside the tramway. Indeed the line was put down, and a new station built, but there was no separate run-round loop for steam engines, and so the Board of Trade denied permission for it to be used for passenger trains. In the end steam trains only seemed to venture north of St John's Road on the new line to supply the gasworks, but it was all soon swept away by the building of the new Joint Line.

Back at St John's Road, which was now the terminus of both the IWR and R&NR, R&NR trains used the original platform, while IWR trains used the island platform where new waiting rooms and toilets had been constructed. In 1879 the island platform was again rebuilt in wood, and a footbridge added in preparation for the arrival of the Joint Line.

Above: On 20th July 1938 W16 *Ventnor* departs with a heavy train for Ventnor, the corrugated-iron carriage and wagon shop built in 1876 can be seen in the background. (Photo: Norman Glover Copyright F.A. Wycherley)

Construction of the Joint Line began in 1878, and by 1879 the bridge carrying St John's Road over the railway and Monkton Mead Brook was completed. Working between Ryde St John's Road and Ryde Pier Head began in July 1880 following alterations to the track layout north of the station to gain Board of Trade approval. A new North signal box was built, with a 23-lever frame, to the same design as that at Esplanade.

Into the twentieth century five gas lamps were erected in the yard at St John's Road in 1904. Further improvements at the works saw the machinery converted to electricity in 1917, while in 1915 a siding was added for the use of IWCR.

Passenger receipts were respectable, amounting to £7,841 4s 4½d (£7,841.22) for the year in 1923, with 24,486 tickets being issued during the busiest month. During the same year 250 tons of general goods were received monthly along with 3,190 tons of coal and coke.

With the Grouping of 1923 the Southern Railway decided to concentrate locomotive work St John's Road, where the workshops were re-arranged with new machines being transferred from Newport. The windmill was demolished along with the chimney from the boiler which originally supplied the machinery.

Meanwhile in the station the platforms were rebuilt in concrete and raised to a standard height with concrete fencing and nameboards, while a water crane was added to the island platform. The station buildings were also altered to provide better facilities. At the south end of the Up platform a 'new' signal box was provided. This was actually re-located from Waterloo East, and opened in December 1928 when both the old South and North signal boxes were closed and demolished, save for the base of the North box which was roofed over and used as a store.

In the goods yard the sidings were re-arranged, and the old goods shed demolished. Instead a new locomotive running shed was built. This had two roads, and was built from concrete with a frame which was made from redundant LBSCR overhead electric gantries roofed in asbestos. To the west was a coal stage served by two sidings, one for locomotives, and another raised one behind for

Above: A general view of Ryde St John's Road in 1949. Note the missing signal arms on two of the dolls of the bracket signal, one of which appears to be in front of the signal box. This is in connection with summer-time double-line working to Smallbrook Junction with the signal arms being re-instated for the winter timetable.
(Photo: Lens of Sutton Collection)

Above: The driver of a goods train with W35 *Freshwater* in charge surrenders the token to the signalman at St John's Road on a wet 5th January 1966.
(Photo: A.E. Bennett Copyright transporttreasury.co.uk)

Right: Inside St John's Road signal box in 1960. Above the lever frame is the plan of the lines the box controls, and on the right by the door is a token machine.
(Photo: Adrian Vaughan)

coal wagons. Meanwhile the old locomotive shed was demolished as the new facilities came into use in May 1930. Later developments saw a new three-road workshop building being provided east of the station in 1938, again making use of second-hand parts. The Island's railways were pioneers in recycling.

St John's Road also handled a significant number of passengers, as well as goods traffic. Figures from *Southern Railway Magazine* indicate that in 1938 193,100 tickets were collected at St John's Road, and that 22,635 tons of coal were received.

Blackout restrictions during the Second World War contributed to an accident at St John's Road, when the driver of W16 *Ventnor* collided with some empty coaching stock in April 1940. Ex-LBSCR brake third No.4167 was damaged beyond repair, but there were no injuries. One of the most major incidents of the war occurred at St John's Road later the same year on 5th December when an exploding bomb derailed the locomotive on the 6.35pm departure from Ryde Pier Head for Ventnor. Fortunately again no one was injured, and the lines were reopened the next day.

SOUTHERN RAILWAY.

COPY.

LONDON (WEST) OPERATING AND COMMERCIAL DIVISIONS.

Acting

Office of Assistant for Isle of Wight,

TELEPHONE: XX 2429.
NEWPORT 93.

L.W.D. SUPT., WOKING.

NEWPORT, I. OF W.   6th. Decbr., 1940.

RYDE ST.JOHN'S ROAD - DAMAGE TO LINE BY ENEMY ACTION, 5/12.

Confirming telephone messages. I have to report that during the operation of a "Red" air raid warning at about 6.40pm yesterday, the 6.35pm passenger train from Ryde Pier Head to Ventnor (Engine No. W.18, O.2 class, Driver P. Vallender, Ryde Depot) became derailed approximately 40 yards north of Ryde St. John's Road Station owing to a bomb pitching and exploding on the Down Main Line immediately in front of the approaching train. The train consisted of four bogie coaches. The Driver managed to pull up and came to rest with the bomb immediately between the driving wheels and the leading wheels of the bogie, and the engine was derailed leading, driving and leading bogie wheels. There was no crater, and at the time it was thought that the bomb was a delayed action one, and, therefore, road services were instituted between Ryde Esplanade and Brading, and Ryde Esplanade and Haven Street as it was found that the bomb had slewed the Up road slightly out of position, and single line working was, therefore, not possible.

A.R.P. Control at Ryde and the Police were advised immediately, and examined the bomb at 8.15pm and reported that it had exploded, and train services were again resumed as between Brading and Ryde St.John's Road, and Haven Street and Ryde St. John's Road, Southern Vectis buses running between Ryde St. John's Road and Esplanade Stations.

At daylight today the Up line was slewed into position, and the train detached from the engine and shunted clear of the running roads. Up trains were then worked over the Up Main and Down trains through the Down Loop. The first train to pass over the Up Main was the 7.50am from Cowes being sent through under caution at 5 miles per hour, and the first train to travel over the Down Loop was the 9.15am from Ryde Pier Head to Ventnor.

The rerailing of the engine is still in progress, also repairs to the road, about six lengths of 30-ft. rail having been damaged in the Up and Down Main Lines. Signal and telephone wires, track relays, etc. were also damaged.

Immediately the train had come to rest passengers were detrained and taken to the shelter at St.John's Road Station; no complaints were made regarding injury, and no further reports have since been received.

So far as can be seen at present there is no damage to the engine, but some glass in a few compartments was broken.

Further details will be sent you later.

(sgd) G.H.R. GARDENER.

P.S. The engine has since been rerailed at 2.55pm today, and repairs to the track are in progress.

Report from the Acting Assistant for the Isle of Wight Mr Gardener concerning the bomb incident on 5th December 1940.

Left: Inspecting the damage from the collision involving W16 *Ventnor* during the blackout on 7th April 1940. The carriage, not surprisingly, was a write-off. (Photo: IWSR Collection)

Following the war and Nationalisation there was a gradual running down of the works at Newport, and the concentration of work at Ryde. Therefore, to provide additional accommodation a concrete sectional building was moved from Newport to Ryde, which was to suffice until work began to prepare for electrification.

Above: W28 *Ashey* makes a fine sight as steam exhausts from its drain-cocks as it moves off-shed on 27th February 1965, with W21 *Sandown* standing at the water crane on the left.
Below: On the coaling stage as an O2 is loaded with coal ready for its next turn of duty in December 1966.

(Both Photos: David J. Mitchell)

1866

Station Building

Goods Shed

Carriage Shed

Locomotive Shed

To Ventnor

Monkton Mead Brook

Plans of Ryde St John's Road in 1866 & 1908
Based on Ordnance Survey Maps

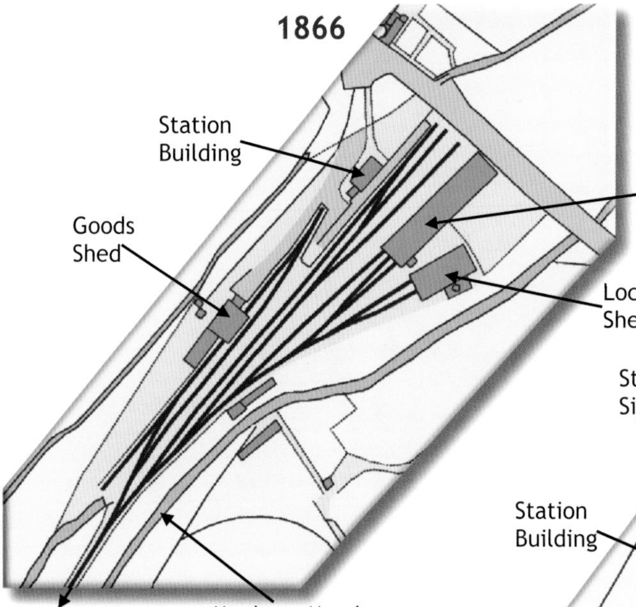

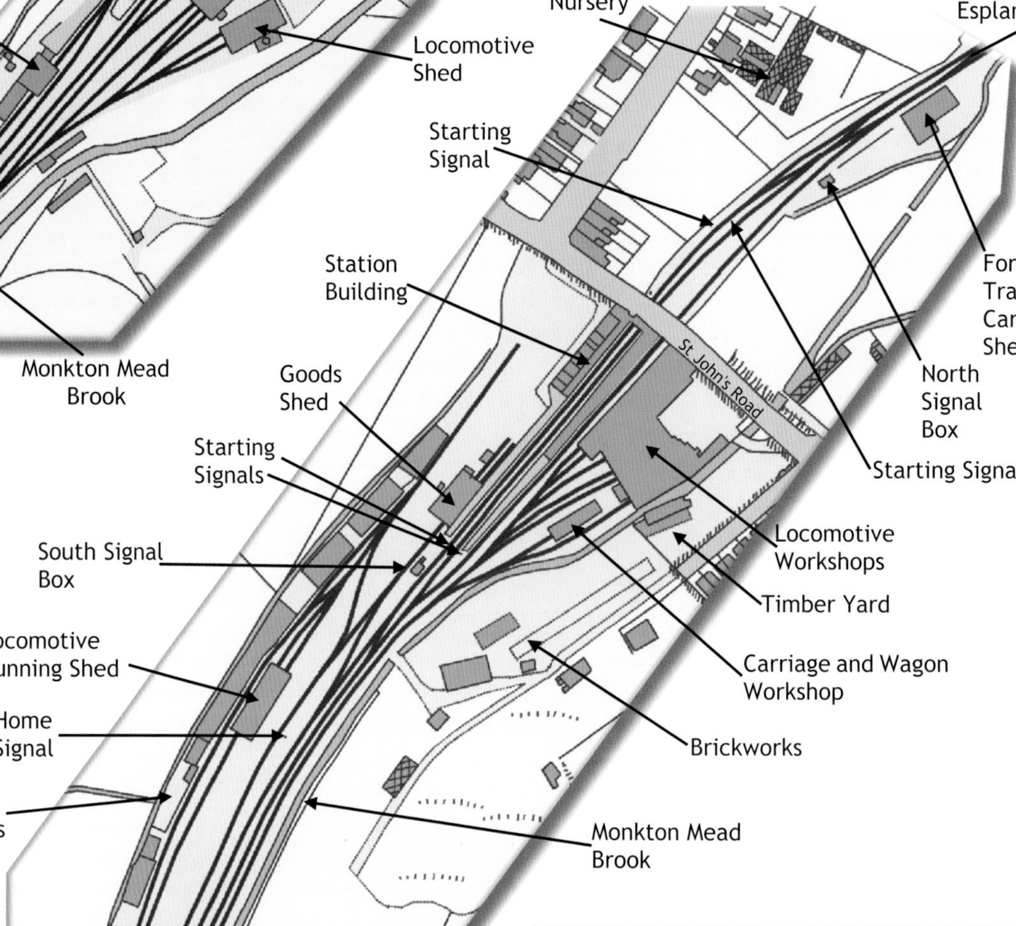

1908

Nursery

To Esplanade

Starting Signal

Station Building

Former Tramway Carriage Shed

North Signal Box

St John's Road

Starting Signal

Goods Shed

Starting Signals

Locomotive Workshops

South Signal Box

Timber Yard

Locomotive Running Shed

Carriage and Wagon Workshop

Home Signal

Brickworks

Coal Staithes

Monkton Mead Brook

Home Signals

Kiln

To Smallbrook

SOUTHERN RAILWAY.

Stock (748K) (1/24)

FOR REPAIRS

From_____ Yard

To_____ Yard

At_____ Station.

Date_____

Examiner.

Any unauthorised person removing this Card from the wagon to which it has been attached will render himself liable to criminal prosecution.

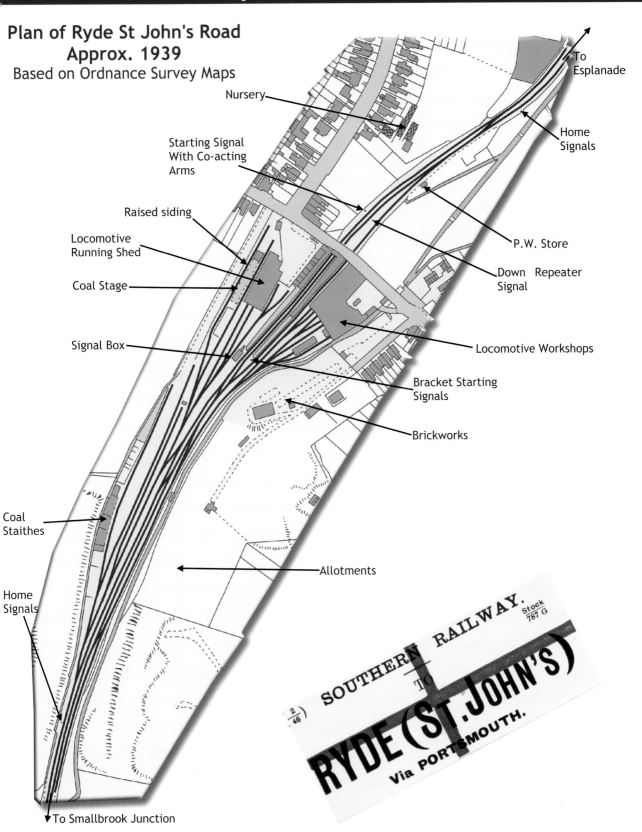

Plan of Ryde St John's Road
Approx. 1939
Based on Ordnance Survey Maps

Nursery

Starting Signal
With Co-acting
Arms

Raised siding

Locomotive
Running Shed

Coal Stage

Signal Box

Coal
Staithes

Home
Signals

To Esplanade

Home
Signals

P.W. Store

Down Repeater
Signal

Locomotive Workshops

Bracket Starting
Signals

Brickworks

Allotments

To Smallbrook Junction

SOUTHERN RAILWAY.
Stock 787 G
TO
RYDE (ST. JOHN'S)
Via PORTSMOUTH.
2/46)

Above: Inside the new engine shed in the early 1930s with W25 *Godshill* and the recently arrived second W9 *Fishbourne* behind. (Photo: IWSR Collection)

Below: W29 *Alverstone* receives attention while a boiler makes a strange sight sat on a trolley outside the works in May 1952. (Photo: S.C. Townroe Copyright Colour-Rail/BRS1573)

Above: A rare view looking south from the bracket signal at St John's Road showing the station throat as a train arrives from Ventnor with the coal staithes to the right, and a fine assortment of wagons and coaches in the sidings.
(Photo: IWSR Collection)

Below: W14 *Fishbourne* heads south from St John's Road with a Ventnor train in June 1961.
(Photo: D.M.C. Hepburne-Scott Copyright Colour-Rail/BRS1568)

Above: With winter single-line working in force O2 W31 *Chale* climbs away from Ryde with the 9.18am train from Ryde to Cowes on 29th October 1965. (Photo: P.F. Bloxam)

Right: In August 1965 the double-track is in use. W33 *Bembridge* has passed under Smallbrook Lane bridge heading for Ventnor, and is now approaching the Down Home signal for the junction at Smallbrook. (Photo: David J. Mitchell)

Smallbrook Junction

Above: In July 1964 the driver of W35 *Freshwater* prepares to accept the token for the line to Brading from the signalman at Smallbrook, who would be standing on the corresponding wooden platform on the other side of the box to that seen in the picture for the Cowes line. (Photo: Copyright Colour-Rail/71303)

From Ryde St John's Road the line climbs on gradients varying between 1 in 135 and 1 in 230 passing the site of a siding which existed between 1866 and 1875. It then passes under Smallbrook Lane bridge before coming to Smallbrook Junction three-quarters of a mile from St John's Road.

For the first fifty years that trains from Newport and Ventnor converged near Smallbrook Farm, there was no physical connection between the tracks of the former IWR and R&NR (later IWCR). The two lines running parallel to St John's Road. However, in 1926 the Southern Railway decided to make it a junction, providing a scissors crossover and signal box there, to allow an improved summer service and aid time-keeping.

The new signal box opened for the summer timetable on 18th July 1926, enabling the line to St John's Road to be worked as double-track during the summer, but it had plenty of ventilation as it had no roof, although this was soon fixed. There was also no road access to the cabin, which could be said to be of compact size, with a platform at the north end for the exchange of tokens.

During the winter months the box was closed, and the signal arms controlling the double-line removed, while those for single-line working were reinstated. All this being accomplished in one night. The two tracks then reverted to being two single lines to St John's Road.

With electrification Smallbrook box was demolished and double-line working to St John's Road was made permanent, controlled from St John's Road signal box. However, Smallbrook Junction did gain its own station in 1991 when it became an interchange with the Isle of Wight Steam Railway.

Right: W20 *Shanklin* and W17 *Seaview* start away from the Home signal at Smallbrook with a parcels train for the Ventnor line on 4th July 1964.
(Photo: A.E. Bennett Copyright transporttreasury.co.uk)

Above: David Mitchell has taken advantage of his lineside pass to climb the signal post to get this shot of W17 *Seaview* approaching Smallbrook box with a train from Ventnor in August 1965.
(Photo: David J. Mitchell)

Right: The compact interior of Smallbrook box, note the different shapes of token in the machines for the Brading and Havenstreet sections to avoid drivers receiving the wrong token.
(Photo: IWSR Collection)

Above: The view from Wall Lane bridge as a train for Ryde drifts down the bank from Brading in August 1966.

(Photo: Terry Hastings)

Below: W16 *Ventnor*, this time approaching Brading on 21st May 1956 with the former Bembridge branch curving away on the right and Wall Lane bridge in the left background.

(Photo: A.E. Bennett Copyright transporttreasury.co.uk)

Left: At the end of steam operations an unidentified O2 departs from Brading past the same site as the previous photo under close observation.
(Photographer Unknown)

Below: On the 24th June 1928 W20 *Shanklin* departs Brading bound for Ryde. Note the Distant arm for trains departing from Brading for Brading Quay fixed to the Home signal post for trains approaching from Ryde.
(Photo: F.J. Agar
Copyright P.J. Fidczuk)

Left: Nearly forty years later, in July 1966, W20 *Shanklin* enters Brading with a Ventnor train.
(Photographer Unknown)

Brading

Above: Passing trains at Brading as W16 *Ventnor* waits for W30 *Shorwell* to clear with a Ventnor-line train on 5th September 1964. The Bembridge line track has long been lifted and the bracket Starting signal removed.

(Photo: David J. Mitchell)

After Smallbrook the line climbs on a grade of 1 in 172 stiffening to 1 in 134 through Whitefield woods (where the Pluto pipeline was laid beside the railway to Sandown during World War Two), and then under Truckells overbridge. Having reached the summit of this part of the line, it begins to fall on a grade of 1 in 79 under Rowborough bridge, then over a cattle creep as it skirts the east side of Brading. Now the grade has eased to 1 in 121 as the line passes under Wall Lane bridge, and enters Brading station on a right-hand curve.

When the line was proposed there was much discussion about whether Brading was sufficient of a settlement to deserve a railway. George Young who was to serve as a director of the IWR, as well as the Ryde Pier Company and the R&NR, described it as 'one of the most wretched villages imaginable', hardly flattering. However, in the end it did get a station, which was originally a simple affair with a loop and single platform.

From the north end of the loop ran the line to Brading Quay, which will be dealt with later in this book. Beside the platform a siding ran to a loading dock, while on the platform a single-storey brick station building was provided.

As there was no signal box or block post only goods trains could officially use the passing loop. Later in the 1870s a second platform was built, and further modifications were made to the station during which a stationmaster's house was provided.

With the construction of the branch to Bembridge further facilities appeared. The branch line ran into a new platform road on the other side of the Down platform, where a run-round loop and signal box with a 30-lever frame were provided. There was also a short siding from the loop, all of which

Left: This early view of Brading shows the station building in its original condition, behind to the right can be seen the weighbridge.
(Photo: IWSR Collection)

footbridge. Otherwise the other major development was the completion of the doubling of the line to Sandown in June 1927. After this very little changed at Brading through Nationalisation until the last train ran on the Bembridge branch on 20th September 1953.

was built at a cost of £3,164, and came into use with the opening of the branch. In the late 1890s a footbridge was added between the platforms following complaints from passengers about the dangers of crossing the line.

Perhaps living up to the dismissive attitude of some of those who had objected to Brading having a railway in the first place, the station, along with Wroxall, was one of the quietest on the line. In 1923 it is recorded that annual passenger takings were £2,062 8s 6½d (£2,062.42p) with a monthly total of 176 tons of coal and coke being received. Mind you compared to some of the very lightly patronised stations on the IWCR Brading was like Clapham Junction!

Even then goods trains continued to run to St Helens Quay until the line was lifted in November 1957. But now general decline was the order of the day, particularly following electrification.

By the mid 1980s plans were prepared for the demolition of the buildings, but these were opposed, and the buildings awarded grade II listed status. Today the fortunes of the station have improved with Brading Town Council completing a major restoration of the station building and signal box, returning them to their former glory.

The advent of the Southern Railway brought some initial changes, with the permanent way being relayed along with new signalling, including the provision of a tall-masted Up Starting signal with co-acting arms to overcome sighting problems with the

Right: An early 20th century view of Brading from the south.
(Photo: IWSR Collection)

Plans of Brading Station in 1866 and 1908
Based on Ordnance Survey Maps

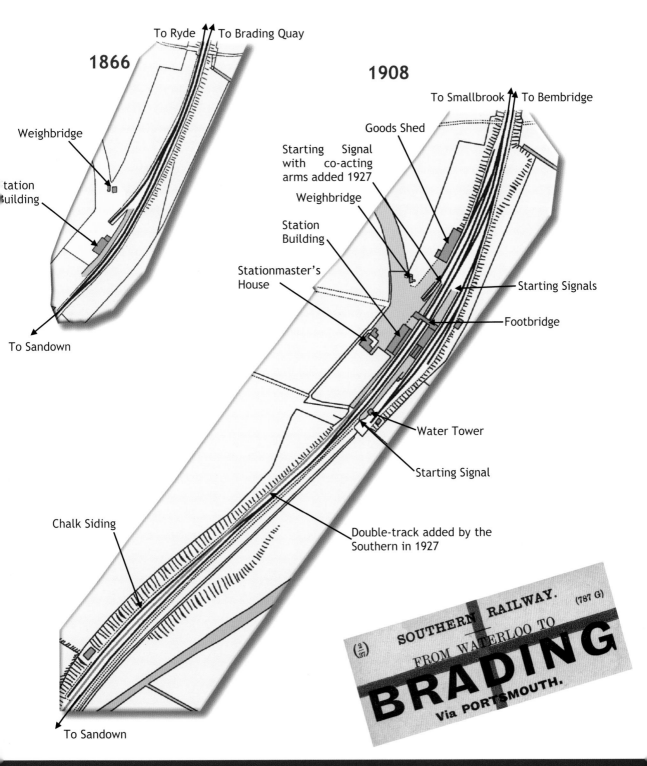

1866

To Ryde To Brading Quay

Weighbridge

Station Building

To Sandown

1908

To Smallbrook To Bembridge

Goods Shed

Starting Signal with co-acting arms added 1927

Weighbridge

Station Building

Stationmaster's House

Starting Signals

Footbridge

Water Tower

Starting Signal

Chalk Siding

Double-track added by the Southern in 1927

To Sandown

SOUTHERN RAILWAY. (787 G)
(2/37)
FROM WATERLOO TO
BRADING
Via PORTSMOUTH.

Above: W20 *Shanklin* arrives at Brading, where passengers are informed they can change for St Helens and Bembridge, with the 12.28pm from Pier Head to Ventnor on 21st September 1951. Beyond the bracket signal can be seen the former cement works at Brading Quay. (Photo: G.F. Bloxam)

Below: The water tower is prominent in this view as W21 *Sandown* arrives at Brading with a train from Ventnor in 1953. On the left of the line the footpath can be seen, which gave photographers access to the line down to Yarbridge. (Photo: J.H. Moss Copyright Colour-Rail/BRS 1459)

Left: Relief signalman Jess Wheeler pulls the levers in the signal box at Brading on 30th December 1966.
(Photo: Terry Hastings)

Right: The restored Brading signal box in May 2010.
(Photo: Alan Doe)

Below: W35 *Freshwater* arrives at Brading in 1963. The Bembridge branch is long gone, and the signal box stands removed from the main station.
(Photo: Adrian Vaughan Collection)

Left: The restored station building in July 2008.

Above: Leaving Brading and heading towards Sandown the line passes the former Chalk siding, which can just be made out in the undergrowth to the left as W27 *Merstone* passes by on 4th June 1966.
Below: On the same date Peter Bloxam is at Yarbridge to take this picture of W35 *Freshwater* passing with its train. The Eastern Yar river is off to the right of this picture. (Both Photos: P.F. Bloxam)

Further down the line at Gills footbridge Peter Bloxam got these two shots of W27. Above it is approaching from Brading, and below earlier in the day it is seen departing Sandown station in the distance. (Photos: P.F. Bloxam)

Sandown

Above: W30 *Shorwell* makes an impressive sight as it stands at Sandown on 27th February 1965. The elevated signal box was one of the most recognisable features of this station, but is sadly no-more.   (Photo: David J. Mitchell)

Departing from Brading trains continue on a downward grade. On the west side of the line was what was known as the Chalk siding. The small workings supplied the cement works at Brading Quay. Shortly after this the line levels, and passes under Yarbridge bridge, at which point the railway is on the flood plain of the Eastern Yar river.

Now climbing again on a grade of 1 in 83 the line passes over a series of bridges including Morton Common, or Sandown Girder, bridge and Sandown Farm bridge. It enters a deep cutting and travels under Gills footbridge before the gradient eases to 1 in 454 as the former line to Newport curved in from the west, and the train enters Sandown station six and a half miles from Ryde Pier Head.

Sandown station, like Brading, was situated well away from the centre of the settlement, and even further from the sea-shore. When the line opened to Shanklin there was a passing loop with a single 200ft platform situated on the Down side of the

line, and a stationmaster's house with an extension housing the booking office and waiting room. Behind the platform a siding led to a loading dock. Later a new Up platform was constructed.

In 1871 new offices were constructed for the IWR's General Manager as an extension to the original building. Meanwhile, the stationmaster was moved out into rented accommodation, which in turn was purchased outright in 1890.

The coming of the Isle of Wight (Newport Junction) Railway (IW(NJ)R) to Sandown led to further modifications to the station layout. A second face was added to the Up platform along with a canopy, to make it an island platform. IW(NJ)R trains terminated on the new platform road where a run-round loop was provided along with a crossover connecting the IW(NJ)R with the IWR. An engine shed was also built in the 'V' between the two lines. Later the Up platform was extended and a wooden footbridge constructed, also a small signal

Left: Probably in the 1880s the station staff pose at Sandown. The station has been altered to accommodate the IW(NJ)R and has acquired a wooden footbridge as well as a signal box. Note both the arches at the bottom of the stairs of the footbridge inscribed with the words that 'Passengers must cross the line by the bridge only', and the signal above the Up shelter. In the distance on the left the IW(NJ)R engine shed can be seen.
(Photo: IWSR Collection)

box was built just to the north of the Up platform.

In the 1880s there were further improvements to Sandown, but the next major change came in 1893, when the platforms were lengthened, this being achieved by the repositioning of a level crossing. The Up platform was widened, with new waiting rooms and canopies, above which stood a raised 32 lever signal box. This controlled a new station layout which included a cross-over to permit direct running from Newport to Shanklin and Ventnor. Meanwhile the footbridge was replaced with a subway between the platforms.

During the early years of the 20th Century various improvements were made including the addition of a public telephone box in 1906, although ironically no public phone was provided for use of the station staff. These new developments reflected the increasing trade at Sandown, and by 1923 the station had annual passenger receipts of £13,029 14s 10d (£13,029.74), with 28,151 tickets being issued in the heaviest month, which also saw 70,016 tickets collected. There was also significant goods traffic with 117 tons of general goods being received at the station every month.

Right: Sandown station building on 31st August 1960. Note the variety of cars on the forecourt.
(Photo: K.G. Carr Collection)

Under the auspices of the Southern, further improvements were made. In 1924/5 steps were taken to improve the clearance between the station-buildings and the platform edge. Later the line between Brading and Sandown was doubled, and preparatory work was begun on doubling the line to Shanklin. In the end this did not happen.

An innovation the SR had developed was the Passenger Luggage in Advance, or PLA facility. With this passengers did not have to cope with heavy cases on their journey. It also reduced the pressure on luggage space on hectic summer Saturdays. This proved so successful that in 1934/5 a canopy was erected over the loading dock to provide an additional covered facility for luggage awaiting collection. Less happy was the death of a porter in July 1934, run-over by a non-stop train on a barrow crossing.

Further improvements occurred in 1938/9 when the Ventnor line platforms were lengthened, the old IWR offices demolished, new toilets built, and the booking hall rearranged. New name-boards were also provided.

During World War Two Sandown suffered a number of incidents, receiving damage on 17th October 1940. Then on 11th April 1941 an unexploded anti-aircraft shell was reported in the Newport loop. Fortunately this proved to be a false alarm. However, the station was damaged again by enemy action in 1944.

Nationalisation did not bring major changes to Sandown until the closure of the Newport line in 1956. Former Sandown stationmaster, Alexander Wheway, recalled that both the final trains were filled to capacity, with the then fledging ITV turning up to film W33 *Bembridge* depart with the last train from Sandown at 7.50pm. On the front of the loco hung a wreath of laurels with the inscription 'In loving memory of a good and faithful servant. Born 1st February 1875, passed away 5th February 1956'. The last train from Newport arrived at 8.20pm with W17 *Seaview* in charge.

In 1957 the Newport line was lifted, but the Newport platform road and some of the sidings were to survive into the electrification era as an engineers' depot, which will be dealt with later. Otherwise the station was largely unaltered until the end of steam in 1966.

Below: Sandown station looking south towards Shanklin in July 2008.

Above: This view dates from 20th September 1926 when the station was part of the Southern Railway, but some lovely period details can be seen. A Newport train waits in the platform on the far left. On the right are the former IWR offices which were demolished in 1938/9.

(Photo: LCGB/Ken Nunn Collection)

Left: W31 *Chale* stands with a Newport line train in Sandown station.
(Photo: C. Woodnutt IWSR Collection)

Below: On 17th September 1953 W36 *Carisbrooke* in unlined black also stands at Sandown with a train for Newport.
(Photo: G.F. Bloxam)

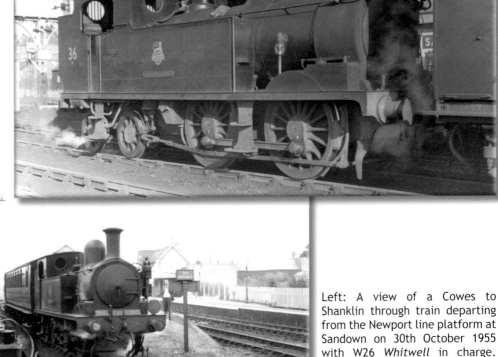

Left: A view of a Cowes to Shanklin through train departing from the Newport line platform at Sandown on 30th October 1955 with W26 *Whitwell* in charge. Note the water crane was accessed by locomotives making use of the short headshunt.

(Photo: A.E. Bennett Copyright transporttreasury.co.uk)

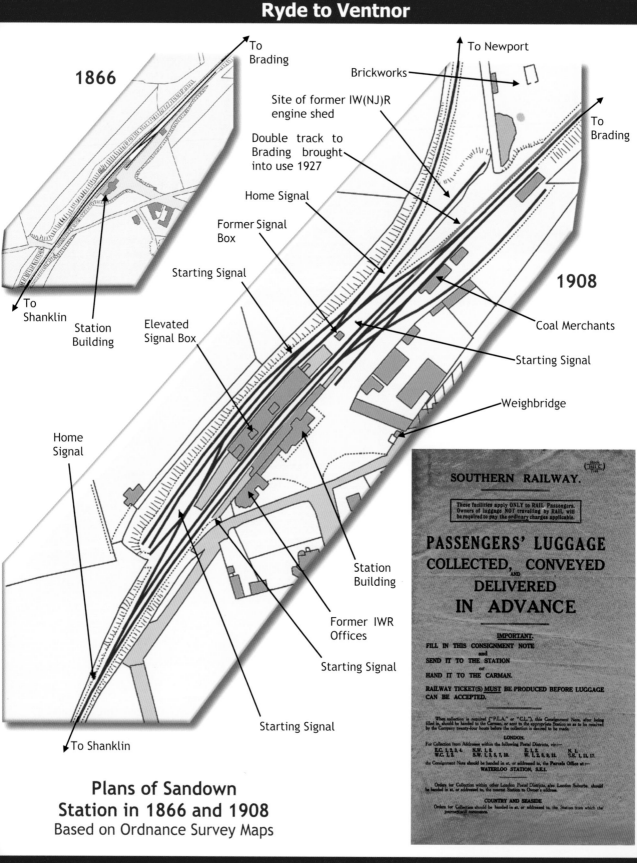

1866

To Brading

To Shanklin

Station Building

To Newport

Brickworks

Site of former IW(NJ)R engine shed

Double track to Brading brought into use 1927

Home Signal

Former Signal Box

Starting Signal

Elevated Signal Box

1908

To Brading

Coal Merchants

Starting Signal

Weighbridge

Home Signal

Station Building

Former IWR Offices

Starting Signal

Starting Signal

To Shanklin

Plans of Sandown Station in 1866 and 1908
Based on Ordnance Survey Maps

SOUTHERN RAILWAY.

These facilities apply ONLY to RAIL Passengers. Owners of luggage NOT travelling by RAIL will be required to pay the ordinary charges applicable.

PASSENGERS' LUGGAGE
COLLECTED, CONVEYED
AND
DELIVERED
IN ADVANCE

IMPORTANT.

FILL IN THIS CONSIGNMENT NOTE
and
SEND IT TO THE STATION
or
HAND IT TO THE CARMAN.

RAILWAY TICKET(S) MUST BE PRODUCED BEFORE LUGGAGE CAN BE ACCEPTED.

Left: Although suffering from some motion blur, this photo is worth including as a rare colour shot of a train arriving at Sandown from Newport with W35 *Freshwater* in charge in October 1954.
(Photo: J.B. McCann Copyright Colour-Rail/BRS975)

Right: A general view of Sandown from the goods yard clearly shows the canopy over the loading dock constructed for the protection of PLA luggage. Meanwhile W21 *Sandown* departs with a train for Ryde on 5th September 1964.

Below: Sandown will always be associated with holiday makers, and here some await the arrival of W30 *Shorwell* on the same date.
(Both Photos: David J. Mitchell)

Left: Once again Peter Bloxam photographs W27 *Merstone*, this time at Los Altos Park on the climb from Sandown towards Shanklin on 4th June 1966.

(Photo: P.F. Bloxam)

Right: Here it is W14 *Fishbourne* heading south towards Skew bridge at Lake on 4th June 1966. Note the scooter in the back-yard on the left, a real period feature!

(Photo: P.F. Bloxam)

Left: W27 once more, on this occasion south of Skew bridge and passing the county ground on the left. Near here was the site of the original Lake Halt.

(Photo: P.F. Bloxam)

Shanklin

At the southern end of Shanklin station W33 *Bembridge* is arriving with a train for Ryde on 2nd June 1963 while W18 *Ningwood* waits in the platform with a train for Ventnor. Note the elevated signal box, which like the one at Sandown was to give the signalman improved visibility. (Photographer Unknown)

From Sandown there is an almost uninterrupted climb on gradients varying between 1 in 85 and 1 in 119, save for a short downward grade of 1 in 107. During the climb the line passes through Los Altos Park before crossing the main Sandown-Shanklin road at Lake. A quarter of a mile further on is the site of what is now Lake station (see page 150). From here the line climbs again passing under Lake Skew bridge.

The line now passes the site of the county cricket ground where a halt had been erected in 1889, and which had latterly served a convalescent home before being closed in 1914. A more recent addition is the Alresford Road footbridge built in 1969, and a half mile beyond this Shanklin station is entered on a 37-chain curve.

Shanklin was the temporary terminus of the line when it opened in 1864. Like many of the other stations on the line it was situated away from the centre of the settlement it was built to serve. The original station layout had a single 200ft platform and a stationmaster's house with extensions on each side, on the Down side of the line. There was a run-round loop which made use of a turntable at the Ventnor end of the station, where there was also a coal stage and water tank.

At the north end of the station were two sidings one leading to a loading dock, with a kickback siding, which served a carriage shed. This shed was not destined to last long, being demolished after the line to Ventnor opened. The opening of the Ventnor line also led to the removal of the turntable, coal stage and water tank.

In 1871 the loop-line was lengthened and a second platform was constructed the following year. This was despite the fact that there was no block post so passenger trains could not cross there.

Isle of Wight Ry.
Series 6)
RYDE
TO
SHANKLIN
SECOND CLASS.
Issued subject to Conditions on
Company's Time Bills.
8 3310 2

Left: Health and safety means very little to the painters, who have their ladder across the Down line in the distance, as a train waits to depart towards Ryde, and the station staff pose for this picture. The date is probably around the end of the 19th Century.
(Photo: IWSR Collection)

Further alterations took place in the 1880s when a platform covering was added, and in 1885 a siding to the gasworks was laid just south of the station on the Up side. Finally in 1892 extensive changes to the signalling permitted passenger trains to pass there. This also involved constructing a subway between the platforms, as well as providing a new 20-lever signal box, which again had an elevated position above the platform awnings to aid visibility. Probably a new booking hall was added at this time, and a tower-like extension on the platform side of the stationmaster's house.

As with Sandown the early years of the twentieth century saw minor changes at Shanklin, with the provision of gas lamps in the goods yard, as well as the extension of the platform awnings. This was to serve the station until Grouping.

It was only to be expected that Shanklin would be one of the busiest stations on the line and the returns of 1923 bear this out. Annual passenger takings amounting to £14,944 6s 8d (£14,944.33), with 36,704 tickets being issued in the busiest month, and no fewer than 72,055 collected. Bearing in mind that goods trains on the line generally only ran at night, the fact that 900 tons of coal and coke were received at the station every month was a significant figure.

The Southern Railway sought to improve Shanklin, and in the mid-1930s plans were made for the station to be rebuilt, possibly in the Southern's 'Odeon' style, but they never came to fruition. Instead alterations were made to the station building to help cope with the crowds of people using the station, as during the three summer months of 1937 no fewer than 199,010 tickets were collected there. As with Sandown the development of PLA led to a canopy being provided for luggage trans-shipment.

Shanklin station seems to have been damaged twice by enemy action during the Second World War, both incidents occurring in the early months of 1943. The first occurred when four or five bombs fell near the station in the January, killing several people in the surrounding area, but only damaging the station buildings, signal box and platform awnings. February saw the second incident when a high-explosive bomb hit a nearby church, and again caused damage to the station buildings.

Following the war years little work seems to have been done at Shanklin. The gasworks siding was taken out of use on 3rd November 1957. From then on there was gradual decline until electrification. Today Shanklin is simply a single-line terminus, and sadly from here on the train journey from Ryde to Ventnor is only a fading memory.

Right: In this restored photograph *Bonchurch* departs from Shanklin with a goods train for Ventnor on 11th June 1910. Most IWR goods trains ran at night, so this is a rare sighting. The loco carries two couplings a three-link coupling for goods trains, and a screw coupling for passenger trains with continuous brakes. Note the signal, the siding to the gasworks in the left foreground, and the elevated signal box can be seen in the left background.

(Photo: LCGB/Ken Nunn Collection)

Above: Looking north from Shanklin station towards Ryde on 23rd June 1928. Note the angular loading gauge on the bay road, the Saxby & Farmer supplied signals, and the coal merchant's depot just behind the van. However, the nameboards appear to have been updated with SR concrete boards.

(Photo: F.J. Agar Copyright P.J. Fidczuk)

Above: Some trains terminated at Shanklin and here W16 pulls away from its train in August 1965 in preparation for running round after the Ryde service has departed from the other platform.

(Photo: David J. Mitchell)

Below: W29 *Alverstone* arrives at Shanklin in the afternoon light on 26th October 1965 with the 3.25pm from Ryde Pier Head to Ventnor. (Photo: P.F. Bloxam)

Plans of Shanklin Station in approx. 1866 and 1908
Based on Ordnance Survey maps

Approx. 1866

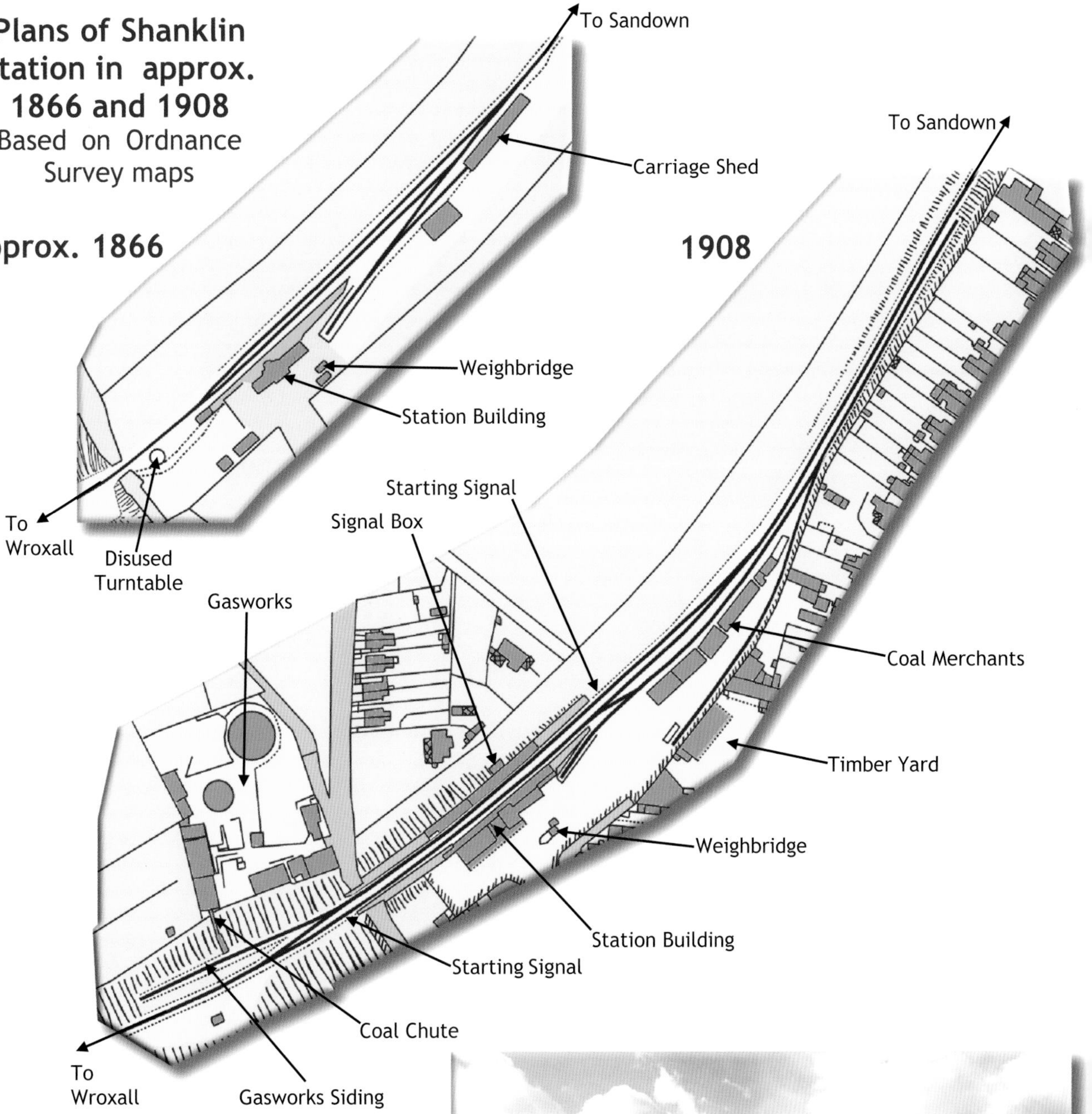

1908

To Sandown

To Sandown

Carriage Shed

Weighbridge

Station Building

To Wroxall

Disused Turntable

Gasworks

Signal Box

Starting Signal

Coal Merchants

Timber Yard

Weighbridge

Station Building

Starting Signal

Coal Chute

To Wroxall

Gasworks Siding

Right: The exterior of Shanklin station in February 2010.

Coal at Shanklin

Left: *Shanklin* passes some loaded coal wagons, as well as a coal merchant's shed and two boys, as it approaches Shanklin with the 9.15am from Ryde Pier Head on 11th June 1910.
(Photo: LCGB/Ken Nunn Collection)

A note from 1895 that a consignment of coal and other goods has been delivered and is awaiting collection from the station at Shanklin.

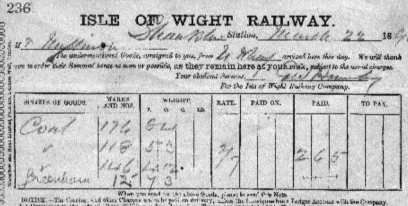

Left: Another customer for coal at Shanklin was the gasworks and here we see E1 W2 *Yarmouth* shunting the gasworks siding in June 1954. The fireman is watching the shunter with his pole which he used to uncouple wagons. From the corrugated-iron structure there was a chute down which the coal went into the works visible to the right of the picture.

The drum which can be seen below the rear buffer beam of W2 is an air tank for the brakes.
(Photo: Copyright Colour-Rail/BRS1188)

Right: Inspecting the damage caused by the bomb that exploded near Three-arch bridge on 12th August 1940. Trains were halted for a number of days while unexploded bombs were dealt with, and the embankment re-built.

(Photo: IWSR Collection)

Below: W22 *Brading* approaches Three-arch bridge with 11.28am from Ryde Pier Head for Ventnor on 29th August 1964. Note the Culver cliffs in the distance around Sandown Bay. This area was notorious for adders, which were a particular hazard for track gangs. The fireman appears to be using the hose which is often seen in pictures of the O2s to water the coal, and so limit the amount of dust that was flying around. These hoses were also used for cleaning the footplate etc. They could also be employed to douse the crews of passing locomotives!

(Photo: Geoff Plumb)

Wroxall

Above: W27 *Merstone* pauses at Wroxall on 27th February 1965. The footbridge was originally at Dean Crossing near Whitwell before being removed in 1926. (Photo: David J. Mitchell)

Almost immediately after leaving Shanklin the line began to climb at 1 in 70 for over a mile and a quarter. This was known as Apse Bank. The line was now heading west and inland in a deep cutting known as Hyde or Sand cutting where there was a siding, passing over Lower Hyde Lane, and under Hyde Road, and Cliff bridges.

Near the top of the bank the IWR built a siding in 1868 to serve a quarry, which became known as Apse siding. It was a lightly constructed affair and locomotives were not permitted to work on it. Also its position on the bank meant that special permission was required for shunting to take place there, which could not be done after dark or during adverse weather conditions.

Beyond the siding the gradient eased to 1 in 228 and the line passed beneath Three-arch bridge, which was an impressive brick-built footbridge. It

was near here that a number of bombs landed on 12th August 1940. One exploded causing damage to the track, two others failed to detonate. The line was closed for ten days (see photo on page 67).

After the bridge the line turned south-west once more, still climbing over Winstone bridge, and past the site of a siding. The gradient increased again to 1 in 113 as the line passed over Yard Farm bridge, and then turned south-east under Wroxall (or Castle Road) bridge to enter Wroxall station.

There does not appear to have been a station at Wroxall when the line to Ventnor opened, as the Board of Trade Inspector's report indicates that the intended station had not been built at the time of inspection. However, by the November the station seems to have been opened consisting of a single stone-faced platform with a wooden single-storey building. North of Wroxall bridge there was a

Before and After

The picture on the left shows Wroxall before the loop-line was installed with the hotel on the right and the station building beyond it.

Below: Looking the other way years later shows that the Down platform was a very simple affair with a waiting shelter and not much else.
(Both photos: IWSR Collection)

private siding to some brick kilns owned by Mr Summerhays, which later became a headshunt for a siding to the local bacon factory. On the opposite side of the main-line the IWR constructed its own general goods siding in 1872.

Beside the station on land sold off by the IWR a hotel was built, which also served as refreshment rooms for the station. Other housing was also built on former railway land around the station.

At some point the station building was re-built, and a headshunt was added to the goods siding by the end of the century. Wroxall was one of the quietest stations on the IWR with an annual passenger revenue of only £1,885 in 1923. Therefore, it is perhaps not surprising that it was the first station where the IWR appointed a woman as stationmistress in 1918, but she did not remain there long, resigning only three months later.

It was the Southern that was to make the greatest change to Wroxall when, in order to

increase line capacity, it authorised the construction of a passing loop there. This came into use on 8th July 1924 along with a second platform. The speed of the construction was probably aided by the use of plans originally prepared by the IWR.

As was usual on the Island the signalling was second-hand, in this case lattice-post signals with London Chatham and Dover Railway (LCDR) finials. The lever frame was placed in the booking office,

as would later be done at Haven Street. In 1926 a footbridge was erected across the platforms and again this was re-cycled, this time from Dean Crossing on the Ventnor West line. One innovation was the provision of Electric Staff Block Instruments, again positioned in the booking office. These were changed for Electric Key Token machines in 1957.

After the re-building, Wroxall became a busy crossing point. In 1935 the bacon factory siding was taken out of use. On 28th September 1940 a bomb fell near the track at the station, but caused no damage to the line. Otherwise Wroxall was largely unchanged until the last passenger trains ran through it on the evening of 17th April 1966.

Plans of Wroxall Station in approx. 1866 and 1930
Based on Ordnance Survey Maps with additions by the author

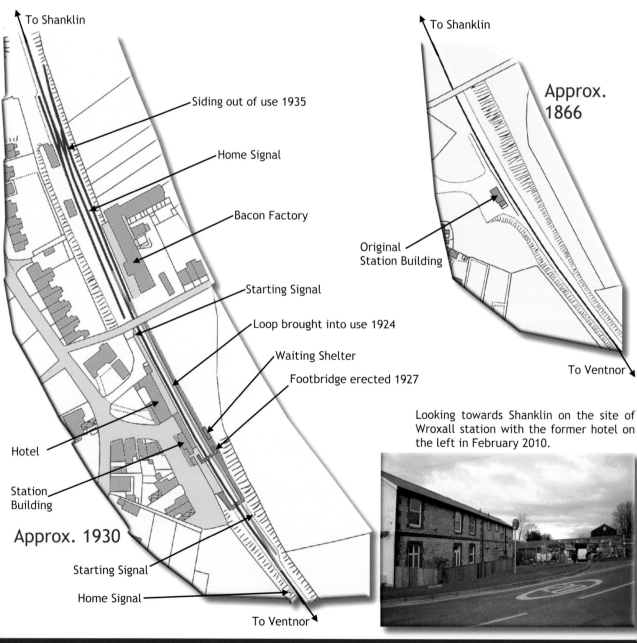

To Shanklin

Siding out of use 1935

Home Signal

Bacon Factory

Starting Signal

Loop brought into use 1924

Waiting Shelter

Footbridge erected 1927

Hotel

Station Building

Approx. 1930

Starting Signal

Home Signal

To Ventnor

To Shanklin

Approx. 1866

Original Station Building

To Ventnor

Looking towards Shanklin on the site of Wroxall station with the former hotel on the left in February 2010.

Above: Viewed from Wroxall bridge at the north end of the station, an unidentified O2 rolls past the old bacon factory with a Ventnor bound train on 18th September 1952.

(Photo: G.F. Bloxam)

Left: The view from the same bridge in February 2010.

Right: The driver of W17 *Seaview* prepares to surrender the train staff as it arrives at Wroxall with the 4.16pm from Ryde Pier Head to Ventnor on 18th September 1952.

(Photo: G.F. Bloxam)

Left: Getting ready to depart as the driver of W33 *Bembridge* takes the token for the single-track section to Shanklin from the signalman at Wroxall on 16th May 1964. Note that the Starting signal has already been pulled 'off' ready for the train to go.
(Photo: F.C. Hammersley)

Below: W27 *Merstone* is photographed by Tony Bennett at Wroxall with a Ventnor train on 20th May 1956. It has been fitted with a Drummond boiler as indicated by the safety valves on top of the dome (see page 126 for more information). (Photo: A.E. Bennett Copyright transporttreasury.co.uk)

Below: On 9th August 1959 W24 *Calbourne* arrives at Wroxall from Ventnor.
(Photo: C.J. Gammell Courtesy Ernie Brack)

Above: W17 *Seaview* waits for W21 *Sandown* to arrive at Wroxall with the 4.42pm from Ventnor to Ryde on 18th September 1952. Of particular note in this picture are the pylons of RAF Ventnor which are still in place on St Boniface Down in the distance. This was one of the very first Radar stations in the country, and played a key role in the Second World War.
(Photo: G.F. Bloxam)

Left: A child's view of trains crossing at Wroxall with W26 *Whitwell* arriving there with a train from Ryde. The number '3' attached to the lamp-iron is the loco duty number.
(Photo: Courtesy Ernie Brack)

Left: W20 *Shanklin* passes under Wroxall Tunnel road bridge before entering the tunnel with a train from Ryde on 20th May 1956.
(Photo: A.E. Bennett Copyright transporttreasury.co.uk

Right: The North portal to Ventnor Tunnel seen from under Ventnor Tunnel road bridge on 20th May 1956.
(Photo: A.E. Bennett Copyright transporttreasury.co.uk)

Left: The North portal in June 2010.
(Photo: Alan Doe)

Ventnor

Above: There are many photographs of this scene at Ventnor with ash being cleaned from the smokebox of locomotives while they take water. However, this one is included because of the level of activity, or rather inactivity, taking place as out of six workers in the picture only two are doing any work! W29 *Alverstone* is the locomotive being serviced on 26th October 1965. (Photo: P.F. Bloxam)

From Wroxall the line continued to climb south-east on a grade of 1 in 88 as it approached Wroxall Tunnel road bridge and the summit of the line at 310ft above sea level. Shortly after this the line entered the 1,312 yard tunnel under the Downs to Ventnor, twelve and half miles from Pier Head.

During the construction of the tunnel the gangs digging from opposite sides of the Downs celebrated the joining of the bores by holding a mass brawl. Later, when the tunnel was in use, gongs were placed near the Ventnor end, which were used by the signalman to communicate with locomotive crews shunting in the tunnel. In 1923 the Southern also fitted two-aspect colour-light signals inside the tunnel, to replace a signal gantry just outside the tunnel entrance.

The story of Ventnor station starts long before the advent of the railway, as the site was a quarry which dated from 1841 at the latest, and was possibly worked by prisoners of war from the

Napoleonic wars. Local legend has it that they were responsible for hollowing out the caves in the cliff faces.

Therefore, the railway found that this was a site

A lamp-post sign that used to direct travellers to the station. (Photo: Terry Hastings)

Left: IWR Beyer Peacoc *Sandown* is seen at Ventno c1900. Something seems to hav damaged the side tank as ther appears to be a series of 'pit marks above the rear driver.
(Photo: Copyright Nationa Railway Museum/SSPL

Vaughan Williams is reputed to have made use of it Another facility was the 'five-minute bell' used to warn weary passenger toiling up the hill from the town of the impending departure of a train.

that they could utilise with very little opposition from the local community, save for those who felt that at 276ft above the sea it was inconvenient. Even then the site had to be enlarged by use of explosives and steam excavators. Further stone extraction, which started in 1867, also increased the area available for expansion over the years until quarrying stopped in 1923.

When the line opened in 1866 the station was incomplete, with temporary wooden buildings, a short narrow platform, run-round loop and bay road, as can be seen in the top photo on page 78, but facilities were gradually improved. 1869 saw the provision of a water tank and crane near the turntable. Later in the same year a new booking hall and waiting rooms appeared. Other alterations in the 1870s included extending the platforms, connecting both the bay road and original goods siding to the turntable, and the construction of a stone-built goods shed in 1876 as well as a signal box in 1877.

Construction began on an electricity generating station next to the station in 1899. This led to the laying of an electric cable through the tunnel in 1904 to supply power to Wroxall, which is apparently still in-situ.

Probably one unique facility was the provision of a sedan chair for the use of those coming to frequent one of the convalescent homes in the area, to convey them from the train to waiting road transportation. On one occasion the composer

Further development of the station was now restricted by the size of the quarry floor, which in turn restricted the length of train that could use the station. Already locomotives had to enter the tunnel mouth when running round their train, which was to continue for the life o the station.

By Grouping in 1923 Ventnor's annual passenge income amounted to a healthy £13,718 with 26,050 tickets being issued during the busiest month. In addition, some 480 tons of coal and coke were delivered every month, and 138 tons of genera goods. One particularly busy week was that of the Ventnor Carnival, and on 27th August 1924 no fewer than 10,000 people were carried.

Given the restrictions of the site, the Southern changed relatively little at Ventnor, although the usual concrete nameboards, and lamp-posts a well as improved toilets and parcels office were provided. Another early change was the remova of the turntable and its substitution with conventional points to allow O2 tanks to run-round

A major blow to the freight traffic came when the electricity station closed in 1928. However, in 193: the sidings were rearranged to accommodate the 'new' bogie coaches that had arrived on the line Later in the 1930s the station was re-painted with improved lighting, and again more covered space for luggage. One other event of note was a drought which occurred in August 1934, when water had to be brought by pipe through the tunnel from Wroxall to supply the locomotive water tank.

Right: A view from the buffer stops on 25th June 1928. The new points are in place, and also note the phone box on the extreme right.
(Photo: F.J. Agar Copyright P.J. Fidczuk)

Below: Ventnor station building in 1962. The phone box has now been replaced with a more familiar design.
(Photo: H.W. Robinson Copyright J.F. Hyde Steam Archive)

One of the first Radar stations was built on the Downs above Ventnor, and this meant that during the war the area became a target for German bombing when the quarry caves were used as shelters. Six bombs were recorded as having fallen on the Downs on 16th August 1940, but although the station was closed there was no damage. On the 22nd August another bomb exploded above the tunnel. Finally an exploding flying bomb in 1944 broke some glass in the station-master's house.

Ventnor was to remain relatively unaltered, but still very busy, through Nationalisation up until its closure on Sunday 17th April 1966. Large crowds gathered to watch W14 *Fishbourne* with the last departure at 8.30pm, and the last arrival in the hands of W24 *Calbourne* at 10.10pm. Both trains being accompanied by a deafening cacophony of exploding fog detonators. Unfortunately, a long battle to save the line from Shanklin had come to nothing. There would be trains no more on this part of the line, a situation which sadly remains to the present day.

The Development of Ventnor

Courtesy of the Isle of Wight Steam Railway Archive here are two prints showing the development of Ventnor during its first ten years.

Left: Dating from shortly after the line opened the temporary station is seen. Note the narrowness of the site at this time.

Right: Probably from the around 1875 the main station building is in place and the goods siding connected to the turntable, but the bay platform is still a terminal road, and there is no goods shed.

Left: Moving forward this 1906 postcard view shows the goods shed and canopies on both the main and island platforms. St Boniface Down rises behind the station. Note how much bigger the site has now become.
(Commercial Postcard)

Above: W27 *Merstone* emerges from the tunnel mouth at Ventnor on 27th February 1965. Due to the restrictions of the site engines running round needed to enter the tunnel in order to clear the points. In IWR days there was a signal gantry over the line by the signal box.

(Photo: David J. Mitchell)

Right: Ventnor signal box in 1962. This was originally supplied by Stevens & Co. in 1877.

(Photo: H.W. Robinson Copyright J.F. Hyde Steam Archive)

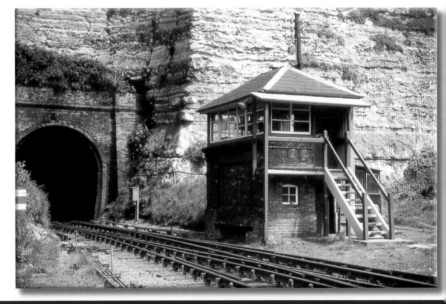

Plans of Ventnor Station in 1908 and 1939
Based on Ordnance Survey Maps

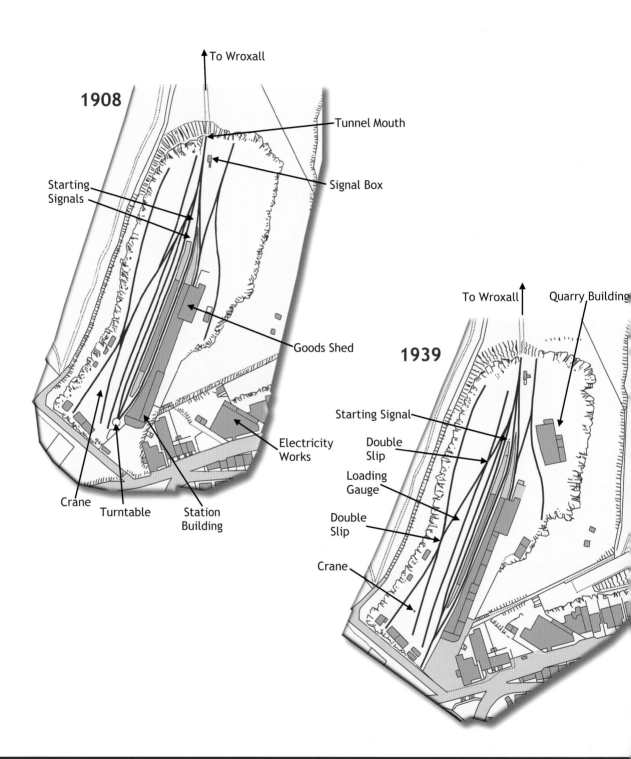

1908

To Wroxall

Tunnel Mouth

Signal Box

Starting
Signals

Goods Shed

Electricity
Works

Crane

Turntable

Station
Building

To Wroxall

Quarry Building

1939

Starting Signal

Double
Slip

Loading
Gauge

Double
Slip

Crane

Above: A traditional vantage point was to climb the Downs above the tunnel entrance, and it is from here that David Mitchell photographed the station in August 1965 with W20 *Shanklin* preparing to depart. Note the caves in the cliff face on the right, which were rented out to coal merchants, the stone-built goods shed, as well as the Austin car.
(Photo: David J. Mitchell)

Right: To gain access to the island platform a moveable bridge was employed which passengers could cross. A system of bell-codes allowed communication between the signalman and station staff as to when it could be safely deployed. It is seen here on 5th September 1960.
(Photo: K.G. Carr Collection)

Above: An activity that was once an everyday occurrence was the loading and unloading of the mail sacks. Here the Royal Mail's Morris Minor Van is backed right up to the van doors to facilitate the process while W27 *Merstone* wait to return to Ryde on 27th February 1965. (Photo: David J. Mitchell

Below: Near the end: W27, with its nameplates removed to prevent them being stolen, departs from Ventnor o 9th April 1966. Ventnor would only see steam for a few more days before the tracks would grow rusty. (Photo: P.F. Bloxam

The Bembridge Branch

By Alan Doe

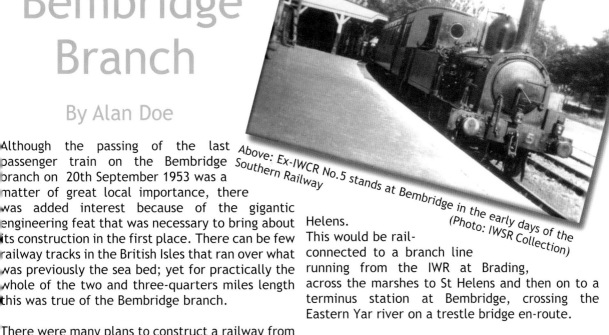

Above: Ex-IWCR No.5 stands at Bembridge in the early days of the Southern Railway
(Photo: IWSR Collection)

Although the passing of the last passenger train on the Bembridge branch on 20th September 1953 was a matter of great local importance, there was added interest because of the gigantic engineering feat that was necessary to bring about its construction in the first place. There can be few railway tracks in the British Isles that ran over what was previously the sea bed; yet for practically the whole of the two and three-quarters miles length this was true of the Bembridge branch.

There were many plans to construct a railway from Brading to Bembridge, with The Bembridge Railway, Tramway and Pier Act 1864 receiving Royal Assent on 29th July 1864 to build a railway from a junction with the IWR at Yarbridge along the south side of Brading Haven to a terminal at the eastern end of Ducie Walk at Bembridge. However, no construction work took place and little more was heard of the scheme.

Brading Harbour Improvement and Railway Company

It was the Liberator Building Society, under the Chairmanship of Jabez Balfour, later M.P. for Tamworth, that had the vision to develop Brading Haven. The scheme, under the title of the Brading Harbour Improvement and Railway Co. (BHI&RC), was to totally transform the area by building an embankment from St Helens to Bembridge thereby closing off the majority of Brading Haven from the sea. Meanwhile the Eastern Yar river was to be straightened and 800 acres of land drained for agriculture. On the seaward side of the embankment a new harbour would be formed, named Bembridge Harbour, with a quay at St Helens.

This would be rail-connected to a branch line running from the IWR at Brading, across the marshes to St Helens and then on to a terminus station at Bembridge, crossing the Eastern Yar river on a trestle bridge en-route.

Stations were to be built at St Helens and Bembridge and a large hotel built on the point outside the terminus at Bembridge. The company also planned to run a steamer service to the mainland from the pier at Bembridge. This enterprise was purely commercial with the aim of making money for the investors of the Liberator Building Society. It was a grandiose scheme, typical of the time when railway companies were spreading throughout the country and investors, often falsely, had the impression that easy fortunes were to be made. In short it was a speculative development.

Construction

In December 1876 the company bought the whole of Brading Haven from the trustees of the late Sir Henry Oglander. Work was then begun on reclaiming the estuary. Sluices at St Helens would allow the flow of the Eastern Yar river to sweep the new quays free of silt to minimise dredging. Construction also began on the railway with two similar station buildings being built at St Helens and Bembridge in 1877. Brading station was

Left: W13 *Ryde* heads towards St Helens past South Quay in approx. 1929/30. Note the headcode for the Bembridge branch at this time. In addition the coaching stock had an interesting background as the first coach was the carriage part of ex-IWCR steam railmotor No.1, while the second was an ex-Midland Railway coach bought for IWCR railmotor No.2.
(Photo: IWSR Collection)

enlarged to accommodate trains from the BHI&RC, and construction of the new line proceeded towards St Helens.

Reclaiming the seabed was not without incident. Under the direction of engineer Mr James Walker, who later became engineer-in-chief of the River Tyne, work started in 1875 on the embankment that was to cut off the estuary from the sea. Thousands of tons of chalk, rubble and clay were brought from Bembridge Down by horse and cart, and from Portsdown Hill, north of Portsmouth, by boat to construct the embankment. Despite the great difficulty encountered in closing the gap in the embankment the sea was eventually shut out on 26th June 1879. To celebrate the completion a cricket match was played on the reclaimed ground, but there are no recorded details of the teams or the result!

This proved premature because disaster struck on the morning of Sunday 18th October 1879, when the sea breached the embankment at a point where Bembridge Sailing Club now stands. An extra high spring tide caused a five to six foot flood over the reclaimed land, which swept away everything in its path including thousands of tons of chalk, tree trunks and a steam pile-driver. After two attempts to mend the embankment, the sea was finally shut out again on 23rd February 1880.

The embankment was then widened to 35 feet at the top and a road, connecting Bembridge to St Helens, made on it at a total cost of £10,000.

It was not to be until 25th May 1882 that Col. Yolland R.E. of the Board of Trade could inspect the completed line to Bembridge. In his report he found that the railway '...commences in an end on junction with the Brading branch of the Isle of Wight Railway near Brading Quay and terminates at Bembridge, a length of 2 miles 14.3 chains (the distance to Brading Quay). The line is single throughout with sidings at a Brick Yard, at St Helens station and at Bembridge.'

His report suggests that with no level crossings, a maximum gradient of 1 in 100 and the sharpest curve of 12 chains that the construction was relatively simple, the line being on an embankment for much of its course. The only major engineering feature would have been the 44 yard wooden trestle bridge over the Eastern Yar river.

Col. Yolland concluded that the whole line was in good order. This was not surprising, as an IWR letter of 15th May 1882 suggested that the line had been used for goods traffic between St Helens and Brading since 1st August 1878. The scheme, along with the construction of the Spithead Hotel at

Bembridge, was financed by Jabez Balfour's Liberator Building Society at a cost of £420,000.

Opening ceremonies took place on Saturday 27th May 1882 with the locomotive *Bembridge* pulling the first train being driven by Mr George Toogood from Ryde. The new railway made a considerable difference to lives of people living in St Helens and Bembridge, the latter growing into a major tourist village and St Helens into a significant port.

From its opening the Bembridge branch was worked under contract by the IWR. The BHI&RC was never financially sound and was in receivership from its earliest days. In 1892 the Liberator Building Society failed. After investigations into the Company finances Jabez Balfour, who had fled to Argentina where he was arrested, was tried for fraud and convicted, being sentenced to a long term of penal servitude, part of which he served at Parkhurst Prison on the Island. The BHI&RC changed its name to the Brading Harbour and Railway Company (BH&RC), and under the terms of the Isle of Wight (Brading Harbour Railway) Act of 1898, the IWR was authorised to take over the company lock, stock and barrel for £16,500 from the 31st July that year.

The Isle of Wight Railway

The IWR ran the Bembridge branch up until the Grouping of the railways of the British Isles on 1st January 1923. Frank O'Brien Adams remembered the village and railway at about the turn of the century, in the years 1900-1902. He recalled that the stationmaster was a Mr Beech and that Bill Vallender was the engine driver, while the guard was Mr Henry Wheeler. Close to the station were three public houses; the *Pilot Boat*, the *Marine Hotel*, and the *Prince of Wales*. Five minutes before the train was due to leave, the stationmaster or porter would ring a bell which could be heard away up in the village. The engine driver and fireman could then generally be seen emerging from the *Pilot Boat*, opposite the station yard, having had their half pint. Driving and firing a locomotive was hot work!

Southern Railway

Grouping had little immediate effect on the branch. The branch train still made the requisite number of round trips during the day, shunted the yard at St Helens Quay and brought an air of permanence to the eastern end of the Island. At

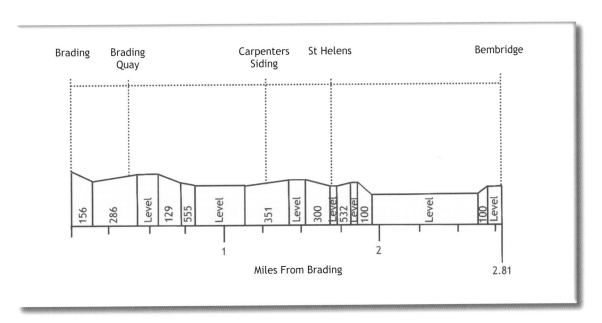

Gradient Map of The Bembridge Branch
Based on a Gradient Map from the IWSR Archive
(Gradients in Form 1 in x)

this point it had yet to be improved to take the heavier LSWR Class O2 engines which were arriving on the Island. Initially the Southern employed some of the ex-IWCR locomotives to work the line including Nos.5 and 8, while later still some of the ex-IWR locomotives were used on the line, usually just before they were withdrawn from service.

The General Strike in spring 1926 was a serious affair. On the Island the SR endeavoured to maintain essential services, and by the second week, starting on Monday 10th May, had instituted four return workings between Ryde Pier Head and Ventnor between 8.00am and 6.20pm. Connecting with these trains were five services from Brading to Bembridge and four in the opposite direction. Considerable distinction was given to the branch during the strike as Lord Herschell, Lord in Waiting to King George V, volunteered to become engine driver on the branch. His home was in Bembridge and he had as his fireman Mr A. Vernet, his chauffeur, who had driven virtually every crowned head in Europe at that time.

Improvements were made to the branch during the late 1920s and 1930s. St Helens Quay was rebuilt as was the bridge at St Helens carrying the road and railway over the Eastern Yar river. By 1932 all the ex-IWR locomotives had been withdrawn, and now duties on the branch were shared by two ex-IWCR class Terriers, W11 and W12. At the outbreak of the Second World War the SR had only three standard classes of locomotives on the Island; the

LBSCR Class A1X; Class E1 and the LSWR Class O2 All but the heavier Class E1 engines W1 to W4 inclusive were allowed to work on the branch.

During the war there were a few incidents on the line; bombs fell near St Helens in November 1940, and again in 1944, while Bembridge station suffered broken windows in January 1941. However, with the coming of peace in 1945 there was an immediate post-war boom. Locomotives were quickly painted bright malachite green and worked hard all through the summer season.

British Railways

After the 1945 General Election, when the Labour Party swept to power, the Government was committed to nationalising the railways. This occurred on 1st January 1948. It is perhaps sad to say that from that day the Bembridge branch, along with other lines, was under financial scrutiny for closure. In the early 1950s car ownership was becoming more widespread and bus services more flexible and competitive. The days of the branch were numbered.

It was in February 1951 that the first closure of the Bembridge branch took place as a result of a national coal strike. The closure lasted just six weeks, but the line would only last another two years before services finally ceased.

In the last year the formation of the branch train was as follows. W14 *Fishbourne* was usually in charge, invariably running bunker first from Brading. Coaching stock was normally provided by push-pull set No.505, of LBSCR

Left: Muscle power is used to turn W13 *Ryde* on the original turntable at Bembridge in this c1930 view. In 1936 a new turntable was built at Bembridge and for details see page 92.

(Photo: Mike Morant Collection)

Map of The Bembridge Branch
Based on Ordnance Survey Map of 1919

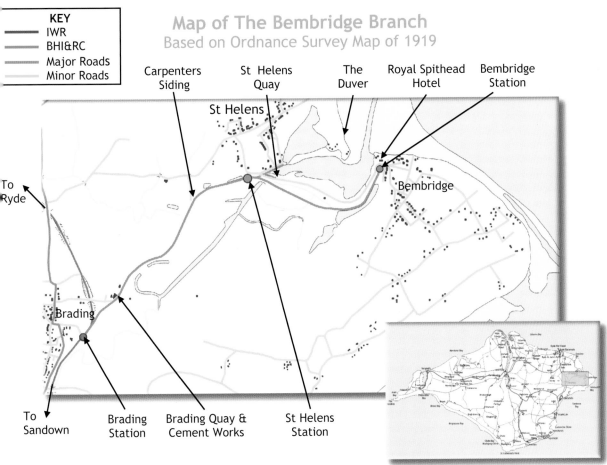

KEY
IWR
BHI&RC
Major Roads
Minor Roads

Carpenters Siding
St Helens Quay
The Duver
Royal Spithead Hotel
Bembridge Station

St Helens

To Ryde

Bembridge

Brading

To Sandown

Brading Station

Brading Quay & Cement Works

St Helens Station

origin, while variety was introduced by the use of an ex-SECR composite coach when additional seating was required. Neither *Fishbourne* nor, when deputising W15 *Cowes*, were suitably equipped for push-pull working so the advantages this could bring were never achieved.

Closure

John Howard Whitehouse, Warden and founder of Bembridge School, proclaimed "I never thought that it would fall to me to make an announcement of a piece of folly unequalled in my experience.........the proposals of British Railways are going to increase considerably the dangers on the Island roads". Nevertheless, and with considerable Island disgust and debate, the line closed from Monday 21st September 1953.

The last train ran on the day before, Sunday 20th September, leaving Bembridge at 9.14pm. Villagers turned out in large numbers to ride on it

including Mr Herbert Occomore, who, for many years was Bembridge Harbour Master and Pilot, and had travelled on the first passenger train ever to run from Brading to St Helens.

Since closure many changes have taken place. Up until the late 1950s carriages were stored and broken up on St Helens Quay, which was gradually closed to commercial shipping. Meanwhile the harbour was sold to the newly formed Bembridge Harbour Improvement Company under the terms of the Pier and Harbour Order (Bembridge Harbour) Confirmation Act of 31st July 1963.

However, the toll road along the embankment was owned and controlled by the British Railways Board until taken over, and the toll abolished, by the Isle of Wight County Council on 25 October 1971. Bembridge station was demolished in the early 1970s as was the Royal Spithead Hotel in 1989. However, there is still much to see of the original track bed that once crossed the sea floor.

Left: W14 *Fishbourne* was the usual motive power on the line in its last year, here unusually it is seen with a single coach train at Bembridge. The driver was Nelson Parsons, fireman Roy Dyer, and the guard Sammy Wells. Note the early BR lined black livery where the top edge of the lining on the bunker was level with that on the side tanks.

(Photo: Terry Hastings Collection)

Left: Tolls continued to be collected on the road from St Helens to Bembridge even after the closure of the railway. Here the Toll Collector stands at Bembridge ready to collect money from traffic using the road.

(Photographer Unknown)

Bembridge

Above: In July 1951 W15 *Cowes* is seen at Bembridge with the train for Brading. Behind the locomotive cab the roof of the signal box is visible, while The Royal Spithead Hotel can be seen behind the station building.

(Photo: Pursey C. Short Copyright Colour-Rail/BRS 878)

The rail-side facade of the station building at Bembridge with its six dormer windows is, architecturally, the more impressive and the side which intending passengers would see as they descended the hill from the village. On the eastern gable of the building was its construction date, 1877, which was several years before the line reached Bembridge, and five years before it was opened. Interestingly the similar building at St Helens is reversed with the plainer side overlooking the platform. Possibly the architect wished to impress the would-be travellers, because here again the more imposing side of the building looks up the hill, Station Road, to the village.

A fence curved around the small turntable at the end of the platform. Why a turntable was required is not clear; normally a point would enable the engine to run round its train to again attach itself to the front of its coaches for its return journey to Brading. Probably a turntable was used because of the lack of space between the end of the platform and the road.

Some have speculated that the station was built with the platform on the wrong side of the station

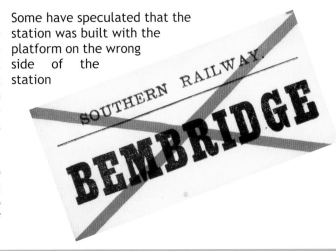

Above: A fascinating view of Bembridge taken c1911, when the IWR had taken over. Ex-BHI&RC saddle tank *Bembridge* stands in the platform with a passenger train, while in the siding wagons are being unloaded into horse-drawn carts. The signal box can be seen above the second coach. (Photo: IWSR Collection)

building. All the windows, look out onto the platform, while at the rear of the building, facing the harbour, there was not a single window.

However, another possible explanation of this peculiarity is that the BHI&RC originally intended to build the railway on the other side of the station building, similar to St Helens, but found that the run-round points would be immediately outside the Spithead Hotel, then under construction, and would require at least two engine lengths beyond the platform. So they re-routed the railway to the south side, and because of the lack of space, introduced the fan turntable, which was more expensive to build and was to cause no end of trouble for drivers.

At first the station had no canopy so people waiting on the platform would be forced to use the waiting room in inclement weather before getting into the train. At the Brading end of the station building was a wooden signal box which controlled the points at that end of the run-round loop and those from the main line into the coal siding. There is no evidence of signals in early photographs.

The stationmaster and his family would have lived in the rooms on the first floor of the station building, while the ground floor would have been devoted to railway work. At the Bembridge end of the building the stationmaster's office can be seen in early photographs; there would also have been a booking hall, waiting room, parcels office and ladies room, while a gentlemen's toilet was provided at the Brading end of the platform.

As well as the stationmaster there would possibly have been a booking clerk, a parcels clerk who dealt with incoming and outgoing freight, a porter who might have helped with shunting, a signalman and a messenger boy. A similar number of staff would have been required at St Helens station and more, perhaps up to 20, would have been needed at St Helens Quay to handle the goods traffic and to work the harbour, making the BHI&RC a major employer in the locality. To the north-west of the station building was the entrance to the toll road connecting Bembridge to St Helens; a new and important route-way at that time.

The Spithead Hotel

Jabez Balfour also financed the Spithead Hotel, which was adjacent to the railway station at Bembridge overlooking the Duver, the harbour and St Helens Roads, a truly idyllic situation. However, t had not always been like that. Behind the Point, n a backwater, seaweed often collected and then lecayed giving off a foul smell. Villagers petitioned he BHI&RC to improve the situation. In 1881 the ompany built a large concrete tank (sic) over this rea, on the site of which H. Ingram and Sons of 'entnor built the hotel.

he hotel was opened on 15th July 1882 when a arty, consisting of Balfour who was the chairman, long with the directors and others interested in he undertaking, travelled from London to 'ortsmouth where they embarked on the paddle teamer *Alexandra* and sailed direct to Bembridge. his was reported to have been the largest vessel o call at Bembridge up to this date. A special rain, adorned with flowers and bunting, was run rom Bembridge to Brading, where further guests nd a military band joined the train and returned o Bembridge for the customary celebration lunch.

oon the hotel had to be enlarged, by the levelopment of the top floor with dormer vindows, to accommodate the many rich and amous who came to Bembridge for sport, specially sailing and golf. Across the harbour on St lelens Duver The Royal Isle of Wight Golf Club, the irst on the Island, was established with an additional room on the side of the hotel becoming he clubhouse.

Queen Victoria reportedly bestowed the title *Royal* o the hotel in 1883, the full name *Royal Spithead Hotel* being written over the entrance porch. It was hoped hat the hotel would help stablish Bembridge as a major ourist resort, and this in turn vould bolster the fortunes of he BHI&RC. Sadly this was not o be.

nto the 20th Century

ome development occurred at Bembridge under the IWR's urisdiction. A brick lean-to vas added at the eastern end of the station building, and at the turn of the century a new siding was added parallel to the run-round loop. As part of their purchase of the BHI&RC's assets the IWR also owned much of the land on the harbour side of the station on which boat sheds were constructed. These were leased by the Bembridge Yacht Club.

After passing into Southern ownership in 1923 Mr Charles Anderson came to the Island to take up the newly-created post of Assistant Divisional Operating Superintendent. His job was to amalgamate the Isle of Wight Railway and the Isle of Wight Central Railway into a single integrated system. As part of this challenging task he set about making a detailed plan of the signalling arrangements on the Island before any substantial alterations were made. These he recorded in a series of beautifully drawn maps which still exist in the care of the IWSR. A record of the Bembridge branch was of course made as part of this, and the following description of the station is based on what Mr Anderson discovered in 1924.

At the station the layout was very simple, consisting of a 220ft long platform with a fan turntable at the eastern end giving a run-round loop of 231 feet. Two sidings were provided; one to the coal stage of 120 feet north of the main line and one to the yard to the south from the run-round loop.

Above: A rare view of the harbour side of the station building showing the austere facade presented to the travelling public. (Photo: E. Dash)

Turn round times, often brief, demanded quick work. The engine was uncoupled and moved forward onto the turntable. Having balanced the engine centrally the driver assisted the fireman in turning the table until it joined up with the run-round loop. Rejoining the engine the driver released the brake and drove off towards the departure end of the station leaving the fireman to replace and lock the turntable ready for the next trip.

While the engine was on the turntable the guard went to the signal box, unlocked the lever frame with his Annett's key, and operated the points at the St Helens end of the station to allow the running round to be completed. Coupling up was performed by the fireman after which the automatic Westinghouse brake was tested and the train held by the engine hand brake until the 'right away' was received from the guard. Meanwhile he had relocked the frame and returned to his van.

Locked points controlled the entrance to the coal and coke siding on the north side of the line. A general merchandise siding was provided alongside the run-round loop. There was no goods shed; a covered van was used for that purpose. On this siding a coach was often stabled to be used when traffic demanded. Two covered vans used respectively as a mobile workshop and tool store also occupied this siding when required. The station had no crane but a pile driver was often to be found in the yard.

At the St Helens end of the station building there was a wooden signal box. It is obscured in most photographs of the time by the station canopy which extended along the front of it. Until 1921 Bembridge was fully signalled, but the signal box was still used as a ground-frame after the signals were removed.

During the winter of 1936 the fan turntable was replaced. A few years before, the line between Brading and Bembridge had been upgraded to take the Class O2 tank engines that were brought over from the mainland. However, the fan turntable at Bembridge was too small to take them, and so smaller locomotives had to be employed. The existing turntable was therefore replaced with one

Above: W19 *Osborne* stands on the replacement turntable at Bembridge on the 10th April 1939. As can be seen it's a snug fit.
(Photo: J.F. O'Neill Copyright The Stephenson Photographic Collection)

Plan of Bembridge Station
Based on Ordnance Survey Map of 1939

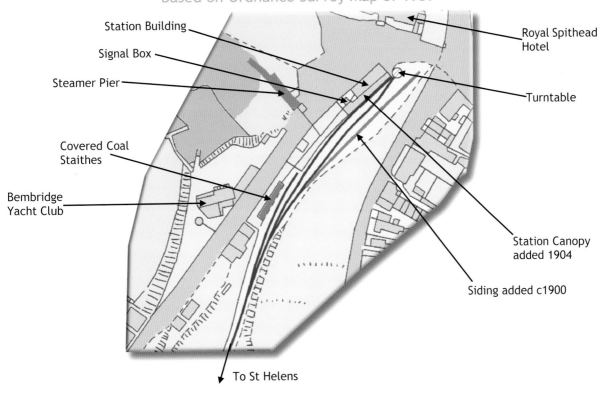

Station Building

Signal Box

Steamer Pier

Covered Coal Staithes

Bembridge Yacht Club

Royal Spithead Hotel

Turntable

Station Canopy added 1904

Siding added c1900

To St Helens

25ft in diameter, just big enough to take the larger engines.

While the turntable was out of action push-pull set No.484 worked the branch with one of the *Terrier* tanks. The turntable also had the distinction of being the only one on the Island at that time, and so it was also used to turn engines when they needed to be sent to Ryde Works for overhaul, as the bunker of the engine needed to face onto the back wall of the works on arrival. Using the turntable saved the triangular journey from Ryde to Sandown, Sandown to Newport and then Newport to Ryde via Haven Street in order to turn the engine.

This proved to be the last major alteration to the station until the last passenger train ran on 20th September 1953.

Right: Two gateposts are the sole remains of Bembridge station in February 2010, with the site of the Royal Spithead Hotel now occupied by apartments behind.

William Weeks

William Weeks became the first stationmaster of Bembridge at the age of 24, after being employed first at Sandown and latterly at Wroxall. Where William Weeks was born is not clear, neither is his exact date of birth known, but it must have been in either 1857 or 1858.

When William left school he joined the IWR at Sandown. He worked hard, served the company well and was noticed by the directors. In either his late teens or early twenties he was promoted to become stationmaster at Wroxall. He obviously did well as he was soon appointed the first stationmaster at Bembridge.

Weeks was an imposing character. He sported a long beard and wore both a frock coat and a splendid gold braided hat. His name was proudly displayed above the waiting room door on the station platform. He married Elizabeth Mary Clayton, a nurse from Shanklin. Their first child, Thomas George Clayton Weeks, was born on 3rd November 1882, shortly after they had moved to Bembridge, and later they were to have two more sons as well as a daughter.

After nine years at Bembridge, and following a long and painful illness, William Weeks died on Sunday 8th November 1891 at the early age of 33 years. His obituary described him as a '..respected stationmaster who through a life of unselfish devotion to duty...had endeared himself to all with whom he was brought in contact.'

He was buried at the parish church at Sandown on 13th November 1891. 'The coffin was conveyed to Sandown by train and was borne thence to its last resting place by platelayers in the railway service.' The IWR was represented at the service by several department heads and five of its eight stationmasters.

This photo shows a number of items of interest, on the left the station building can be seen without a canopy over the platform. In front of the station clock probably stands William Weeks, the first stationmaster of Bembridge, whose life is described above. To the right is the Spithead Hotel, which is described on pages 90 & 91. In front of the hotel is the original turntable, later replaced by the Southern Railway. Note also the boats which have been stored alongside the railway fence.
(Photo: IWSR Collection)

Above: On 20th September 1953, the last day of passenger operations, W28 *Ashey* waits to depart with one of the final passenger trains. The line operated under 'one engine in steam', hence the lack of signalling.

(Photo: K.G. Carr Collection)

Below: The covered coal staithes at Bembridge on 27th April 1953. This was to prevent the wind from blowing the coal dust around.

(Photo: Copyright HMRS J.J. Davis Collection)

St Helens Quay

Above and Below: Ken Carr surveyed the scene at St Helens Quay on 20th September 1953.

Above: Looking at North Quay with the water tower and former engine shed on the right. The vessel tied up nearest to the quay was the dredger *Ballaster*, used to keep the channels clear.

Below: Looking along the South & West quays with one of the rail-mounted cranes. Out of use rolling stock can be seen stored on the quay in the distance.

(Photos: K.G. Carr Collection)

Left: The scene at the quays in February 2010.

Left: *Excelsior* belonging to *Chaplins* is tied up at North Quay with some IWR wagons in the background.
(Photo: IWSR Collection)

Leaving Bembridge in 1924 the line curved right close to a wooded hill where a cap windmill could be clearly seen. The line then ran on its own embankment, inland from the road, to the left of which was a stretch of water known as Bembridge Lagoon, noted for its waterfowl population. Soon the line passed St Helens South Quay before the Eastern Yar river was crossed by means of a steel bridge which had gradients as steep as 1 in 100 on either side, to give the necessary elevation above the water.

St Helens Quay had been transformed with the arrival of the railway, becoming a major goods yard, and for several years the major port on the Island. The quays themselves were designed to accommodate vessels of up to 250 tons and 280ft in length.

Mr Thomas Henry Woodward, of Eastfield, Ryde, regularly drove on the line from 1900 until he retired in 1933, after completing 53 years of railway service. He recalled that shunting on St Helens Quay at night was the most arduous part of his duties. Timber, cement and building materials were among the main imports with coal brought regularly to the gasworks by the steam collier

Allerwash which, along with the *Ellington*, was associated with St Helens for many years. She was built for the Isle of Wight Imported Steamboat Company in 1861 as the *American*. Vessels also delivered oil and glass carboys to the works.

Mrs V. Dyer of St Helens was employed as a clerk by the IWR at the quay. Among her memories are the firms that used the quay; these included *Chaplins*, *Pickfords*, *Curtis*, and *Long's Brewery* as well as the War Department. She also remembered that the dredger was out on most days keeping the channel clear, which also provided sand and gravel ballast for the Island lines.

Chaplins, a local firm, contributed considerably to goods traffic brought in by sea from the mainland. Goods of all kinds were loaded into box wagons, labelled, sorted and then dispatched by the railway. The volume of traffic could be so great that it was often after dark before the goods got away. While shunting was in operation at the quay it would be the job of the junior parcels porter from St Helens station to operate the level crossing gates across the main road to Bembridge. This would mean working until midnight if a lot of shunting was required.

Above: Freshwater, Yarmouth and Newport Railway *Terrier* No.2 and the ex-Manchester, South Junction Altrincham Railway coaches arrive at St Helens in 1913.
(Photo: IWSR Collection)

For a brief period in the late 19th Century a train ferry operated between St Helens and Langston on the mainland near Hayling Island. Commencing operation in September 1885, it only lasted until March 1888. As there are no pictures of 'foreign' wagons on the Island, it suggests that its use was very limited.

From 1903 the gasworks was served by a 1ft 11½in gauge line positioned across Latimer Road leading from the gas house siding to the gas house. This was used to convey coking coal in tubs from the quay to the works where coal gas was made.

By the 1920s St Helens Quay consisted of two wharves; North Quay and South Quay. On the North Quay were the engine house, gasworks and goods shed along with the weighbridge. The weighbridge, as well as the turntable at Bembridge, was maintained by the engineer responsible for 'outside works'. Len Creeth, the engineer, was on 24 hour call out if problems arose. There was also a fan shaped signal by the weighbridge that was used to regulate the movement of the engine when weighing wagons; presented square on it meant 'stop', edge on, 'all right' and waggled to and fro, 'set back'. Meanwhile, on South Quay mobile steam

cranes operated, which could be moved onto small turntable to enable them to serve the 100t road that joined North and South Quays.

Under the SR major improvements were made. The *Southern Railway Magazine* reported that on 23r October 1924 the first half of a new road bridg across the Eastern Yar river at St Helens ha opened to traffic. This had been reconstructed i concrete, enabling vehicles weighing up to fiv tons to pass over it.

St Helens Quay was also rebuilt, including a new layout of sidings, new deep water quays and th rebuilding of the steam cranes. Thes improvements were inspected by the SR Chairman Brigadier General the Hon. Evelyn Baring alon with fellow directors and the General Manager, S Herbert Walker. A special train conveyed the part along the line from Brading to St Helens.

During the 1930s traffic began to decline. By th time of Nationalisation the main use for St Helen was as a means for bringing in supplies for th railway, and for the storage of surplus an condemned rolling stock. This continued until th line to the Quay was finally lifted in 1957.

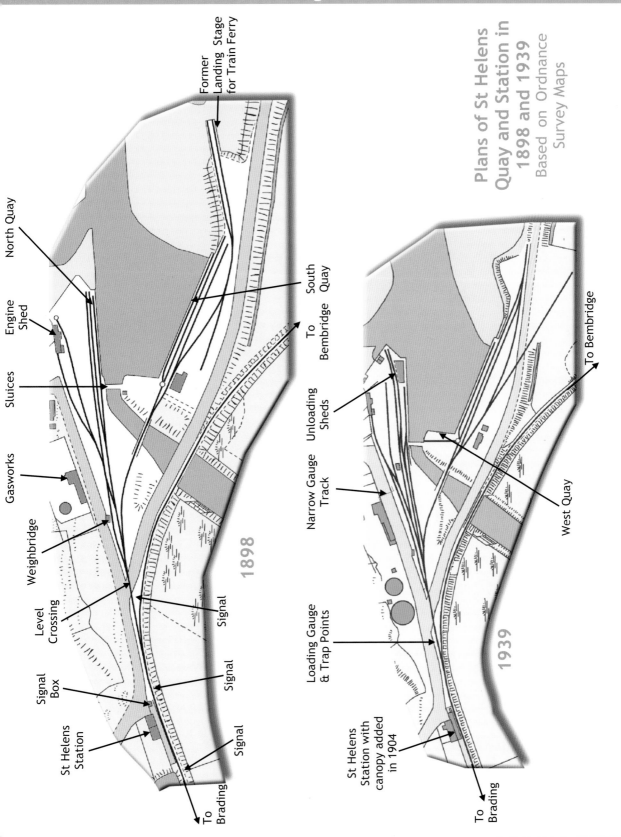

Plans of St Helens Quay and Station in 1898 and 1939
Based on Ordnance Survey Maps

1898 plan labels:
- Former Landing Stage for Train Ferry
- North Quay
- Engine Shed
- Sluices
- Gasworks
- Weighbridge
- Level Crossing
- Signal Box
- St Helens Station
- To Brading
- Signal
- Signal
- Signal
- Signal
- To South Bembridge Quay

1898

1939 plan labels:
- Unloading Sheds
- Narrow Gauge Track
- Loading Gauge & Trap Points
- St Helens Station with canopy added in 1904
- To Brading
- West Quay
- To Bembridge

1939

St Helens

W14 *Fishbourne* again, this time in September 1951 with the 1.57pm from Bembridge to Brading having departed from St Helens.
(Photo: G.F. Bloxam)

After crossing the Eastern Yar river the line then swept round a sharp left hand curve and into St Helens station, which was the only intermediate station on the branch 1.75 miles from Brading. This comprised a single platform on the north side of the line, originally with a ten-lever signal box at its eastern end, which controlled the points to St Helens Quay.

From the main-line the line to the quays passed under a loading gauge and then over the main road by means of a level crossing. This was controlled until 1929, when the signals were removed, by Stevens and Son's flap type signals operated by levers Nos.4 and 7 in the signal box. Another signal was also linked to the catch points which further protected the entry to the main line from the quays.

As has been noted the station building at St Helens was of an identical design to the one at Bembridge, but with the railway on the less ornate side of the building. The single platform was lengthened following an accident in 1902 when a passenger fell when alighting from a train. A canopy was added in 1904, and there was also a water crane at the harbour end of the station. Under the SR St Helens changed little, not even gaining a new nameboard, and except for repainting remained largely unaltered until closure in 1953.

Above: On 14th September 1953, during the last week of operation on the branch, W14 *Fishbourne* rounds the curve into St Helens station. Note the loading gauge and trap points on the line leading to the quays on the left.

(Photo: G.F. Bloxam)

Below: W14 again with a train from Brading on 1st June 1953. Although the stock consists of one of the push-pull sets W14 was not equipped for push-pull working, and so had to run-round its train at each end of the journey.

(Photo: Peter H. Hay)

Left and Bottom: Two views taken by Ken Carr of St Helens station.
Left: On 26th June 1950 W14 is at the station with the 4.45pm train from Brading for Bembridge. Period features are the bus stop and road speed limit sign. The water crane on the platform end can also be seen.
Below: St Helens from the Brading end on 15th September 1953. The gas-holder was a landmark here for many years.
(Photos: K.G. Carr Collection)

Departing from St Helens a train travelled on an embankment curving to the left. About half a mile from the station the train passed the Home signal for Carpenters siding, which in 1924 shared a post with the Distant signal for St Helens for trains approaching from Brading. Carpenters siding was described by Col. Yolland, when he inspected the line on its opening in 1882, as Brick Field siding. This was unlocked by an Annett's key which was kept at St Helens station. It served a small brick works until removed in 1946.

Travelling south-west the line snaked right and left for nearly a mile until coming to Brading Quay. The sidings here served the cement mills, which operated intermittently between 1884 and the 1920s, and in later years were used to store redundant coaching stock.

A small signal box, supplied by Stevens and Son, controlled the sidings and signals, as well as a level crossing. The Brading Quay Distant signal, operated by lever No.1, was, unusually, mounted on the same post as Brading station's Home signals, while the No.3 lever in the frame locked the crossing gates. Mechanical linkage caused the gate lamps to revolve and show their light correctly along the railway or road as necessary, as it was a skew crossing fixed lamps would not project their red lights along line or road.

After Brading Quay the next 43 chains of the line followed the course of the original siding from the IWR main line at Brading. Curving left the line ran parallel with the main-line from Ryde until it entered Brading station.

Left: W14 once more in September 1951 returning from Brading and heading towards St Helens.
(Photo: G.F. Bloxam)

Right: W13 *Ryde* in approx. 1929 poses at the former cement works at Brading Quay with a Billinton designed four-coach close coupled set.
(Photo: Copyright HMRS Ray Chorley Collection)

Left: W20 *Shanklin* is on duty on the branch on 18th September 1952 where it is seen just coming parallel with the line from Smallbrook as it heads into Brading.
(Photo: G.F. Bloxam)

The End of Steam

Photo: Terry
Hastings

The poster on the left signalled the beginning of the end of steam on the Island's railways. British Rail announced the withdrawal of services from the line to Cowes from 21st February 1966, and then between Shanklin and Ventnor from 18th April 1966, while the last train ran from Pier Head on 17th September the same year.

This was of course not unexpected, services on all the Island's lines had been under threat for some time, and enthusiasts had taken the opportunity to come and enjoy the delights of riding behind steam on the Island's railways for a number of years. However, now the final days approached, and passenger steam, at least under the auspices of British Rail, ceased on the Island on 31st December 1966.

Below: The slightly premature *Vectis Farewell* tour of 3rd October 1965 has already been mentioned on page 16. Here the special with W14 and W24 in charge waits for the service train hauled by W28 *Ashey* to depart from Ventnor. Health and safety does not seem to be an issue here.   (Photo: David J. Mitchell)

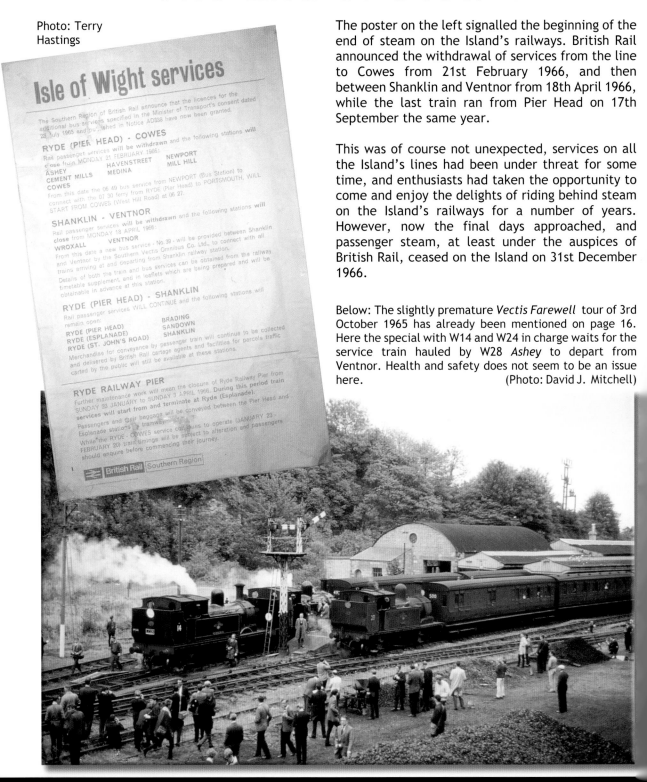

Isle of Wight services

The Southern Region of British Rail announce that the licences for the additional bus services specified in the Minister of Transport's consent dated 28 July 1965 and published in Notice AD338 have now been granted.

RYDE (PIER HEAD) - COWES

Rail passenger services will be withdrawn and the following stations will close from MONDAY 21 FEBRUARY 1966:

ASHEY   HAVENSTREET   NEWPORT
CEMENT MILLS   MEDINA   MILL HILL
COWES

From this date the 06 49 bus service from NEWPORT (Bus Station) to connect with the 07 30 ferry from RYDE (Pier Head) to PORTSMOUTH, WILL START FROM COWES (West Hill Road) at 06 27.

SHANKLIN - VENTNOR

Rail passenger services will be withdrawn and the following stations will close from MONDAY 18 APRIL 1966:

WROXALL   VENTNOR

From this date a new bus service - No.32 - will be provided between Shanklin and Ventnor by the Southern Vectis Omnibus Co. Ltd., to connect with all trains arriving at and departing from Shanklin railway station.

Details of both the train and bus services can be obtained from the railway timetable supplement, and in leaflets which are being prepared and will be obtainable in advance at this station.

RYDE (PIER HEAD) - SHANKLIN

Rail passenger services WILL CONTINUE and the following stations will remain open:

RYDE (PIER HEAD)   BRADING
RYDE (ESPLANADE)   SANDOWN
RYDE (ST. JOHN'S ROAD) SHANKLIN

Merchandise for conveyance by passenger train will continue to be collected and delivered by British Rail cartage agents and facilities for parcels traffic carted by the public will still be available at these stations.

RYDE RAILWAY PIER

Further maintenance work will mean the closure of Ryde Railway Pier from SUNDAY 23 JANUARY to SUNDAY 3 APRIL 1966. During this period train services will start from and terminate at Ryde (Esplanade).

Passengers and their baggage will be conveyed between the Pier Head and Esplanade stations by tramway.

While the RYDE - COWES service continues to operate (JANUARY 23 - FEBRUARY 20) train timings will be subject to alteration and passengers should enquire before commencing their journey.

British Rail | Southern Region

Left: 1966 was a year of gradual decline. The last trains ran on the Cowes line on 20th February, and then on the 17th April the final passenger trains headed up to Wroxall and Ventnor.
Here is W20 *Shanklin* approaching Wroxall Tunnel bridge on that day as it prepares to enter the tunnel for one of the last times.
(Photo: A.E. Bennett Copyright transporttreasury.co.uk)

Below: Ryde Pier Head was the next station to cease to echo to the sound of steam with the last trains arriving and departing on Saturday 17th September. On this date W35 *Freshwater* is seen in the evening light as it prepares to depart.
(Photo: Terry Hastings)

Left: Finally on 31st December 1966 the last steam trains ran between Ryde and Shanklin. Special services were run, and hundreds of people crowded onto them. Here W27 *Merstone*, which banked the last train out of Ryde Esplanade, bears the farewell wreath with the inscription 'Farewell to IOW Steam' and the chalked message on the bunker-side 'Farewell Old Faithful'. An era was indeed coming to a close.

(Photo: Terry Hastings)

Right: On the last day Peter Bloxam recorded the scene at St John's Shed with W22 *Brading* and W27 presenting a sorry sight, while in the background is diesel D2554, which had arrived on the Island on 7th October.

(Photo: P.F.Bloxam)

Below: The sad sight at Newport some months later as W20 *Shanklin* has been put to the cutter's torch.

(Photo: Terry Hastings)

Above: The scene at St John's Road in February 2010 bears little reminder of its past.

Locomotives
Part One: Pre Grouping

The issue of who or what owned which locomotive on the Isle of Wight at a particular time can be convoluted to say the least. Therefore, to save confusion locomotives are detailed with the company whose line they were first associated with upon arrival on the Island.

The Cowes and Newport Railway

No.1 *Pioneer* & No.2 *Precursor*

These were two 2-2-2 well tank locomotives built by Slaughter, Gruning and Co. of Bristol in 1861, and delivered to the Island new at a cost of £1,960 each. They were 19 ton locomotives with 5ft 3in driving wheels, outside cylinders, and no cabs. Delivered in a 'pretty blue tint' with white, black and red lining, they were named *Pioneer* and *Precursor*.

In 1884 & 1886 respectively they acquired stovepipe chimneys, cabs, and a large cylindrical sandbox on the boiler. Under the IWCR they were re-painted into the IWCR Crimson Lake livery. No.1 was fitted with Westinghouse air brake equipment in 1892, when a new boiler and cylinders were also fitted, and No.2 was fitted with air brake equipment in 1894. Under the IWCR the locomotives lost their names, and were known simply by their numbers No.1's nameplate was removed in 1893, and No.2's in 1895.

Above: A familiar view of No.1 after its nameplate was removed. On the back of the author's copy is the information that the driver is 'Fred Smith's father'.
(Photo: Author's Collection)

However, they were rapidly becoming obsolete, and No.2 was taken out of use in January 1901, with No.1 following in the August. They were both scrapped in 1904, save for the boiler from No.1 which was used to power workshop equipment at Newport until 1918.

Above: A splendid view of No.2 taken between 1886 and 1893.
(Photo: IWSR Collection)

No.3 *Mill Hill*

Purchased new for the C&NR in 1870 this was an 0-4-2 saddle tank built by Black Hawthorn and Co, it was even fitted with the luxury of a cab (later enlarged). Supplied with lined green livery and named *Mill Hill* it suffered from being dropped in the water when delivered.

By the end of the century it was being used as a shunter at Medina Jetty where it acquired the nickname of *The Snatcher*. It was then used as the motive power for the IWCR's second railmotor between 1907 and 1913 before seeing further service as a separate locomotive.

After the First World War the price of second-hand locomotives encouraged the IWCR to sell off its obsolete engines. So No.3 was sold and went to Middlesborough, and then to Plenmeller Colleries near Haltwhistle until being broken up in 1930.

Above: *Mill Hill* with its original cab.   (Photo: IWSR Collection)

The Ryde and Newport Railway

Two locomotives are known to have been used in the construction of the R&NR, these were:

Dorothy this was a locomotive that arrived on the Island as *Stuart* and is detailed in the IWC locomotive section (see page 115).

Bee was an 0-4-0 saddle tank purchased new from Henry Hughes and Company of Loughborough in 1875. It was initially used to haul the construction trains, and later for shunting and other work at Medina Jetty. Finally, in 1888 it was sold to R.T. Relf of Okehampton.

No.4 *Cowes* & No.5 *Osborne*

Nos.4 & 5 were 2-4-0 tanks ordered from Beyer, Peacock & Co. for £1,765 and delivered in May 1876. They were numbered in sequence after the C&NR's three locomotives

Above: No.5 repainted into Southern Railway livery as W5 c1925.
(Photographer Unknown)

ut also carried the names *Cowes* and *Osborne* espectively. Being of a more advanced design than he C&NR's locomotives they had 5ft driving wheels nd weighed 26 tons 8 cwt. Their early livery is not lear, but by 1887 and the formation of the IWCR, hey were painted dark chocolate.

Inder the IWCR the locomotives received new aint, but lost their names, No.5's went in 1892, nd No.4 the following year. In general they seem o have given good service, although they had ifficulty in hauling heavier trains. During the First Vorld War like the other locos in the IWCR fleet hey were painted black.

oth survived into Southern Railway days; No.5 ecame W5, being overhauled and repainted into R colours in 1924. It was transferred to Ryde for se on the Bembridge branch. No.4 did not fare so vell not even being repainted into SR livery, and vas scrapped in 1925. Sadly No.5 was only destined o last another year being scrapped in 1926.

No.7 *Whippingham*

he need for new locomotive power to haul eavier trains led the Joint Committee of the &NR, R&NR and IW(NJ)R to purchase a 36 ton 19 wt 4-4-0 tank locomotive from the North London ailway in 1880. It was one of eight locomotives uilt by Slaughter, Gruning and Co., the builders of los.1 & 2, in 1861, but it was rebuilt in 1875 at ow Works. Although purchased on behalf of the oint Committee, it vas listed in Board of rade returns as R&NR roperty, named Vhippingham but etained its lined black ivery.

Inder the IWCR it ecame known simply s No.7, and worked nainly on the Newport- andown line, being itted with air-braking quipment in 1893. In

July 1906 it burst a tube in service. After being deemed to be beyond economic repair it was laid aside.

Isle of Wight (Newport Junction) Railway

During the building of the IW(NJ)R at least two locomotives were used on the line. *Brading* will be featured in the IWR section, where it was used in the construction of the IWR with the name *Stuart* (see page 115). The second locomotive was *Comet*, on hire from the LSWR, but was returned before the line opened fully.

No.6 *Newport*

Newport was originally built as a 2-2-2 well tank for the Whitehaven Junction Railway in 1861 by R. & W. Hawthorn & Co., where it was known as *Queen Mab*. It passed into the hands of the Furness Railway, then the LNWR, before being purchased for use on the IW(NJ)R for £750, and arrived on the Island in 1874.

A cab was fitted at Ryde Works, and the loco was painted in a sandy brown livery. However, it proved somewhat unreliable. In 1881 it was reported the boiler had burst, but it seems to have been kept in use until 1890, finally being scrapped in 1895. Sadly no photos of it appears to have survived.

eft: No.7 at Newport after 893.
(Photographer Unknown)

Left: In this photograph No.
is seen at Newport probabl
around 1920.
(Photographer Unknown

the former IWCR lines
and was withdrawn i
1925.

No.8

No.8 became the last new
locomotive ever ordered
for the Island's railways
save for steam railmoto
No.1, being another 2-4-
tank supplied by Beyer
Peacock in 1898 at a cos
of £1,950. Weighing in a
30 tons 17 cwt with 5f
1inch driving wheels, i
proved to be a very suitable locomotive.

It underwent a heavy overhaul in 1903-4, with new
boiler tubes being supplied in 1911, and a new
firebox in 1914. Otherwise it seems to hav
required little major work. Lasting into St
ownership as W8, it spent its last summer in 192
working the Bembridge line before bein
withdrawn.

Isle of Wight Central Railway

No.6 (2)

The first locomotive to be purchased under the
auspices of the IWCR was a replacement for No.6
Newport. This was a new 4-4-0 tank locomotive
ordered from Black, Hawthorn & Co. and delivered
in June 1890.
Equipped with
Westinghouse air
brakes from the
outset it had 5ft 3ins
driving wheels, and
weighed in at 40 tons.
No.6 proved a
reliable locomotive,
and survived into SR
ownership as W6
(being the only 4-4-0
tank the Southern
ever had on its
books). It was
transferred to
shunting duties at
Ryde, having been
deemed too heavy for
the poor state of the
permanent way on

Above: W8 in SR livery at Newport on 22nd June 1928. Note the *Royal Daylight* tank wago
behind the coal pile, one of the few private owner wagons on the Island.
(Photo: F.J. Agar Copyright P.J. Fidczuk

The Terriers

The *Terriers* were designed by William Stroudley for the LBSCR London suburban services, particularly the South London line where in the space of nine miles there were 11 intermediate stations. They were given the name *Terriers* by *The Engineer* magazine on account of their 'bustling' performance. First entering service in 1872 they were 0-6-0 tank locomotives weighing 24 tons 12 cwt and a Tractive Effort of 7,650lbs. Fifty were built and designated A (later A1) class. Later several were modified with larger boilers and an extended smokebox, being known as A1X class with a Tractive Effort of 10,695lbs.

Above: W9 is seen here during its final weeks of service on 25th April 1926 at Newport with a train for Freshwater composed of one of the ex-LCDR push-pull sets. It had been fitted for push-pull working by this time.

(Photo: LCGB/Ken Nunn Collection)

As they were displaced some were sold to other railways including the IWCR. In later years they became synonymous with the Hayling Island branch, before the last one was withdrawn in November 1963. Happily a number are preserved including four which served on the Island.

No.9

Originally built in 1872 as No.75 *Blackwall*, it became No.9 in the IWCR's fleet in 1899. Surviving into SR ownership it became W9. Early in 1926 it was fitted with push-pull apparatus for use on the Ventnor West branch. However, only a couple of months later it broke a crank axle near Ningwood on the Freshwater line, suffering further damage in the yard at St John's Road while awaiting repair, and was therefore condemned in 1927.

Right: W10 *Cowes* is seen here at Newport c1930 after rebuilding as an A1X, but before it was fitted with steps and handrails in front of the side tanks.

(Commercial Postcard)

No.10

No.10 arrived in April 1900, having originally been LBSCR No.69 *Peckham*, built in 1874. Under the auspices of the Southern it was repainted and numbered W10 in 1925, and was fitted with push-pull apparatus as well as steam heating equipment. In 1930 it was named *Cowes*, and was rebuilt as an A1X with a larger boiler refurbished from W12. However, it was sent back to Eastleigh in 1936, where it was scrapped in 1949.

Left: No.11 is seen here at Newport on 11th May 1919.
(Photo: LCGB/Ken Nunn Collection

on the Hayling Island branch, being withdrawn in September 1963.

It was then sold to *Butlins* as a static display at their Pwllheli holiday camp, remaining there until January 1973. But it was then loaned to the Isle of Wight Steam Railway, restored to static display in 1920 condition, and unveiled in 1975. Purchase from *Butlins* followed in 1976, and finally No.11 returned to steam in 1989, as the only surviving IWCR locomotive.

No.11

Coming to the Island in 1902, former LBSCR No.40 *Brighton* was special as it had been a gold medal winner at the Paris Exhibition of 1878. It became the only *Terrier* on the Island to be fitted with coal rails. These restricted the driver's view in reverse, and so the coal bunker was extended in 1918, as with the other *Terriers*. The overhaul of 1918 also saw it converted to an A1X class with a larger boiler.

Repainted in SR livery in 1924 with the number W11, it was also fitted with push-pull apparatus and steam heating equipment. In 1929 it received the name *Newport*, and was fitted with a Drummond chimney in 1932. Four years later front footsteps and handrails were added.

As part of the 'standardisation' of classes on the Island it was returned to Eastleigh in February 1947, where it was overhauled. It then continued to serve on various parts of the SR system including some months on the Kent and East Sussex Railway (KESR) in 1948. By now numbered 32640 it worked for most of its last years under British Railways

No.12

At the end of November 1903 the last of the four *Terriers* acquired by the IWCR arrived on the Island. This was ex-LBSCR No.84 *Crowborough*, the last of the class to be built in 1880. It was rebuilt with a new larger boiler in 1916 to convert it to an A1X class.

Passing into SR ownership it became the last locomotive to be overhauled at Newport when it was repainted and numbered W12. In 1929 it was given the name *Ventnor*. Finally W12 was sent back to Eastleigh in 1936 where it remained until being broken up in 1949.

Right: No.12 at Newport c1920.
(Photographer Unknown)

No.7 (2)

With the withdrawal of the original No.7 in 1906 there was a gap in the locomotive fleet, which needed to be filled. Therefore, a further Beyer-Peacock 2-4-0 tank of 1882 vintage was acquired in the December, second-hand from the Midland and Southern Western Junction Railway for £695. At 35 tons 5 cwt it was the heaviest Beyer Peacock loco to serve on the IWCR, it was also the first to receive a new variation on the IWCR's livery with simply the initials of the company being painted on the sides of its water tanks.

Above: No.7 at Cowes c1910.   (Photo: IWSR Collection)

Again it lasted into SR ownership, but was not repainted into SR livery. Finally, it was condemned in April 1926 having completed 247,675 miles in Island service.

No.2 (2)

The last locomotive acquired by the IWCR turned into a real white elephant. It was an 0-4-4 tank locomotive built in 1895 at Seaham Harbour Works for the Marquis of Londonderry's railway in County Durham, and bought in 1909 for £750. The clue to its problems lies in its weight at 45 tons 15 cwt, 5 tons heavier than any other locomotive in the IWCR fleet (although ironically it was about the same as an O2 class loco).

This caused problems with the lightly laid IWCR permanent way, and although attempts were made to reduce the weight by cutting down the side tanks and bunker these proved unsuccessful. Therefore, it was confined to use on the Ryde-Newport-Cowes route, and was often out of use. Finally it was sold in 1917 to Armstrong, Whitworth and Co. of Elswick for £1200, so at least the IWCR made a profit, but it only lasted until 1921 when it was broken up.

Left: Because of No.2's short career on the IWCR few photographs of it in service seem to exist, and are often of poor quality. This one shows it at Newport after its side tanks had been shortened.
(Photographer Unknown)

The Steam Railmotors

No.1

Following visits to other lines which employed steam railmotors the IWCR took the plunge and ordered a new unit in 1905 for use on lightly loaded services.

The carriage was made by Hurst, Nelson and Co., and the locomotive by R.&W. Hawthorn, who also assembled it. When delivered in 1906 there were initial problems with overheating axleboxes, and it was not until 1908 that it was ready for service.

Railmotor No.1 on delivery.   (Photo: HMRS John B Denison Collection)

However, after this other factors came into play, not least the growth of third class travel, which the railmotor, with seating only for first and second class passengers, was not equipped for. Therefore in 1910 the decision was taken to separate the locomotive and carriage. The former, after being fitted with an extended frame and enlarged coal bunker, was still known as No.1. In 1918 it was sold for £950 and went to Middlesborough, then to Fourstones Quarry in Hexham where it was later broken up. Meanwhile the carriage became No.52 in the IWCR stock.

No.2

On a wave of euphoria from the arrival of the firs steam railmotor, the IWCR board decided in 190? it needed another. However, this time it became a DIY job with locomotive No.3 *Mill Hill* providing the motive power and a second-hand clerestory carriage purchased from the Midland Railway the passenger accommodation. These were taken into Newport Works for modification. It was never strictly speaking a railmotor, as the two parts were kept separate, but No.3 was covered with sheeting to give an appearance that this was a single unit.

When it entered service in 1909 it proved a failure the 22 ton carriage being too heavy for the locomotive, and it was laid aside in 1912. Finally No.3 returned to use as an individual locomotive in 1913.

Left: Railmotor No.? is shown in a posed shot along the Undercliff on the Ventnor West branch Note the limited look out for the drive riding at the front o the coach.
(Photo: Copyrigh National Railwa Museum/SSPL)

The Isle of Wight Railway

Grafton

This was a contractor's locomotive used on building the IWR. It was believed to have been a 0-4-0 tank locomotive, which had been rebuilt by Hawthorn & Co (Leith) in 1858. *Grafton* stayed on the Island until being auctioned off in 1866, when it was used in the building of the Hayling Island branch before ending its days in Cheshire.

Stuart or Brading or...

Stuart was originally built in 1841 by Bury & Co. before being rebuilt as a tank locomotive by the Glasgow & South Western Railway in 1853, and sold in 1860. Arriving on the Island in 1863, *Stuart* was employed in hauling spoil trains on the IWR. In 1867 it passed into IWR hands and was named *Brading* in 1868.

Next it appeared as a construction engine on the W(NJ)R in 1872, then on the R&NR in 1874 where it was named *Dorothy*, working the first public trains when that line opened. What happened to it next is unclear, it was possibly used in Ashey quarry and/or it found its way back onto the W(NJ)R. From here it was purchased by the SHI&RC when it gained the name *St Helens*.

On the Bembridge line *St Helens* was used to help with construction, and later as a reserve engine. In 1893 it was on the move again to help with the building of the NG&SLR, where it was used at High Hat tunnel under the name *St Lawrence*. The IWCR hired it in 1897 for use at Medina Jetty, before it was finally broken up in 1898, thus ending a colourful career.

Ryde, Sandown and Shanklin

For its opening the IWR ordered five identical 2-4-0 tank locomotives from Beyer, Peacock & Co. This was later reduced to three due to financial issues.

Above: *Ryde* after withdrawal at Eastleigh on 19th August 1934 having just been moved there from the Island.
(Photo: F.J. Agar Copyright P.J. Fidczuk)

Delivered on 20th July 1864 they were unnumbered but named *Ryde*, *Sandown* and *Shanklin*. They had 5ft coupled wheels with inside cylinders and weighed in at 30 tons 9 cwt. Originally they were painted dark chocolate and had no cab. However, weather-boards were fitted later, and in the 1870s they were painted in lined red livery.

They were also fitted with high handrails above the side tanks for the fireman to hold onto while climbing along the side of the loco while it was in motion. These were removed after 1900 when new safety legislation was brought in.

Over the years they had various alterations including the fitting of Westinghouse air brake equipment. Other modifications which changed their appearance came with the repositioning of the dome from over the firebox (see p8) to the centre of the boiler, and the addition of cabs.

After entering Southern Railway service *Ryde* was repainted in SR green, and became W13, retaining its name. *Shanklin* became W14, but sadly *Sandown* had suffered a major frame fracture, and was condemned in 1923. It was broken up without receiving a Southern number. *Shanklin* was taken out of service in November 1927 and scrapped soon after. Meanwhile, a major overhaul in 1929 saw *Ryde* outshopped with a Drummond pattern chimney, and steam heating equipment, but it was withdrawn in 1932.

However, it remained on the Island for another two

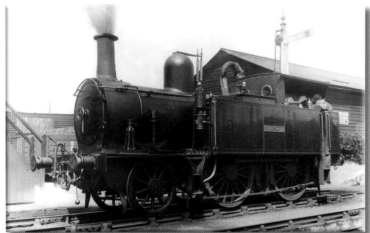

Left: *Ventnor* at Ryde St John's Road c1900, with the original goods shed behind, after a cab was fitted.
(Photo: W. Dunning Copyright R.K. Blencowe)

Becoming part of the Southern fleet as W16 in 1923, it was the last of the original IWR locomotives to remain in service. During an overhaul in 1930-1 it was fitted with the cab from former IWCR No.8, and steam heating *Wroxall* continued to serve at Newport mainly on the Freshwater line services until being withdrawn in June 1933 when it had run 1,350,674 miles.

years, during which time the then Assistant responsible for the Island's railways, A.B. MacLeod, made efforts to see the loco preserved, which will be detailed later. *Ryde* finally moved to Eastleigh in 1934, and, despite hopes it might be saved, was broken up in 1940.

Ventnor

With the IWR's opening to Ventnor there was soon the need for more motive power, and so in October 1868 *Ventnor* was delivered from Beyer, Peacock & Co. Although to a similar design to that of its predecessors, it possessed a rear weatherboard from the outset, although it still had its dome over the firebox, which was later moved to the position seen above.

Becoming W15 under the Southern regime, it was transferred to Newport in 1924. Here it served primarily on the Freshwater line until being withdrawn in 1925.

Wroxall

Growth in traffic led to further orders for locomotives being placed, again to the same basic design. *Wroxall* arrived in April 1872, slightly larger than its predecessors, with 5ft ½in driving wheels and weighing in at 31 tons 12 cwt. It was the first to both have the dome positioned in the centre of the boiler barrel, and to be fitted with a cab, although you cannot please everybody, as crews complained that it restricted the view!

Above: *Wroxall* at Newport on 21st September 1926.
(Photo: LCGB/Ken Nunn Collection)

Brading

Another few years on and traffic demands led to the ordering of a larger version of the 2-4-0 design which arrived in December 1876 and became the second loco to receive the name *Brading* in the IWR's fleet. Weighing in at 34 tons 8 cwt it was significantly heavier than previous locomotives and was to the same design as IWCR's second No.7.

Following Grouping *Brading* received the number W17, and in 1924 was transferred to Newport. In April 1926 it was withdrawn from service.

Bonchurch

The last of the IWR's fleet was ordered in 1882. However, its arrival at the Island was delayed when the barge carrying it sank to the sea-bed off St Helens. There it remained for several days until it was raised again, but it was not seriously damaged and entered traffic on 1st June 1883. With a weight of 36 tons and 4 cwt it was similar to *Brading* but with some design improvements, including an external coal bunker.

Bonchurch proved a most capable locomotive, and with various modifications served the IWR well, entering into Southern ownership as W18. It was finally withdrawn in May 1928 having clocked up 1,326,067 miles during its service on the Island.

Bembridge Harbour Improvement and Railway Company

Bembridge

Scott and Edwards, contractors for the line owned an 0-6-0 saddle tank engine named *Stanley* which they brought to the Island in March 1879. Renamed *Bembridge*, this Manning Wardle Class M engine, works No. 517, had formerly been delivered new in March 1875. Comparable in size to the IWR's 2-4-0Ts it was ideal for working the passenger and freight

trains on the branch, with an occasional ballasting excursion along the main line to Ventnor. It was sold to the BHI&RC in March 1882 for £650 and passed into the hands of the IWR when they purchased the line.

An interesting experiment took place in 1903 when *Bembridge* was converted to oil-firing for a few months. However, this resulted in insufficient savings to warrant the capital expenditure required for further conversions.

In February 1916 *Bembridge* was put into store. Then in April a letter was received from the War Office requesting the availability of any six or four wheeled coupled tank engines. *Bembridge* was inspected by staff from the Office and pronounced satisfactory. A barge was sent on 15th August 1916 to collect it from Ryde Pier Head, and the engine left the Island after working on the Bembridge branch since 1879, a total of 37 years. It eventually went to Fovant Camp near Dinton in Wiltshire. There as No.15, *Bembridge* was employed on the two mile Fovant Military Railway until 1920 when it is thought it was scrapped.

St Helens

For the history of the BHI&RC's other locomotive see *Stuart* on page 115.

Right: *Bembridge* at Brading after the cab was altered in 1911.
(Photo: IWSR Collection)

Freshwater, Yarmouth and Newport Railway

Freshwater

Freshwater was a contractor's loco used in the construction of the FYNR, and also hauled some of the excursion and goods trains to run before the line's opening. It was an 0-6-0 tank locomotive built by Robert Stephenson and Co. in 1880, and arrived in 1887, reputedly painted green.

After the full opening of the FYNR *Freshwater* seems to have been moved to the IWR, before being sold to the London and St Katherine Dock Company. Later still it was employed on the Weston, Clevedon and Portishead Light Railway. *Freshwater* was then sold to the Renishaw Iron Company in Derbyshire where it ended its days in 1937.

No.1

Following the break with the IWCR in 1913, the FYNR acquired a Manning Wardle 0-6-0 Q Class saddle tank of 1902 vintage from the contractors Pauling & Elliot. Before arriving on the Island it may have been overhauled at the Great Central Railway's (GCR) works courtesy of FYNR director Sir Sam Fay. No.1 was fitted with both Westinghouse and vacuum brakes, which meant it could haul all the FYNR's coaching stock.

Above: FYNR No.1 at Hunnyhill c1920. Note the dual air and vacuum brake pipes on the buffer beam.
(Photo: LCGB/Ken Nunn Collection)

Passing into SR ownership in 1923 it was repainted in olive green in May 1924 and given the number W1. After this it was assigned as the shunter at Medina Wharf, and in 1928 was named *Medina*. Finally W1 was withdrawn in June 1932, being shipped back to Eastleigh to be broken up the following year.

No.2

No.2 was another *Terrier* locomotive, this time on hire from the LSWR. Originally built in 1876 as No.46 *Newington*, it had been purchased by the LSWR in 1903 and numbered 734. The LSWR fitted it with a Drummond pattern boiler with its distinctive dome top safety valves. Following the FYNR's purchase of No.2 in 1915, it was repainted in apple green livery.

After Grouping No.2 was given an extended bunker as per the ex-IWCR locos, as well as air-brake apparatus. In March 1924 it was painted SR Green, receiving the number W2. It was overhauled again in 1927 when steam heating, as well as push-pull equipment were fitted. Later it was named *Freshwater*.

The next major alteration for W2 came in 1932 when it was converted into an A1X class, and was also renumbered W8 to allow for the 'new' E1 class locomotives arriving on the Island. In the mid-1930s it was supplied with front steps and handrails.

Above: FYNR No.2 at Newport. Note the safety valves on the top of the dome, a result of being fitted with a Drummond pattern boiler. (Photographer Unknown)

During the Second World War it was repainted in unlined black, and was kept in reserve until being transferred back to the mainland in April 1949. At Eastleigh it was renumbered 32646 and spent much of its final days under the auspices of British Railways working the Hayling Island branch until being withdrawn from service in November 1963. Fortunately this was not the end, and 32646 was preserved at Droxford on the Meon Valley line as the property of the Sadler Railcar Co.

From there it was sold to Brickwoods Breweries in 1966 and moved back to Hayling Island to serve as a sign for the *Hayling Billy* public house. Finally in June 1979 a repainted W8 returned to the Island, having been donated to the Isle of Wight Steam Railway, and was returned to steam in June 1981, as will be seen later in this volume.

Above: The FYNR's Drewry Railcar waits at signals having descended from the viaduct at Newport past the FYNR Yard on 12th May 1919. Note the cattle truck converted from an open wagon on the right.   (Photo: LCGB/Ken Nunn Collection)

Drewry Railcar

The last item in the FYNR's fleet never received a number or name. It was a Drewry semi-open four-wheel railcar fitted with a 20hp engine, and equipped to seat between 12 and 15 people. Arriving in July 1913, the railcar was used for lightly loaded trains, as well as picking up passengers from late running ferries at Yarmouth, earning the nickname *The Lurcher*. Just lasting into Southern Railway service, it was withdrawn in 1924, and finally scrapped in 1927.

The Newport, Godshill and St Lawrence Railway

The only other standard gauge locomotives known to have worked on the Island pre-Grouping, were two engines employed on the construction of the NG&SLR.

Godshill

This was an 0-6-0 tank locomotive rebuilt by Kerr-Stuart in 1895 from an

original locomotive of 1863. After completion of the NG&SLR extension to Ventnor Town it went to work on the GCR Marylebone extension.

Weaste

This loco was constructed as an 0-4-0 tank by Hudswell, Clarke in 1888 and used in the building of the Manchester Ship Canal. Having been used as a contractor's locomotive for J.T. Firbank who completed the Ventnor extension, it then moved on from the Island. In 1901 it was noted as being employed in the building of the Basingstoke and Alton Light Railway, and was finally scrapped in 1922 by the Western-super-Mare Gaslight Co.

Right: The only known photograph of the locomotive *Godshill* with construction workers on the NG&SLR.
(Photo: IWSR Collection)

Locomotives
Part Two: Southern & British Railways

As will have been seen from the previous pages, the Southern Railway inherited a variety of locomotive types when it took over the Island's railways. Therefore, two priorities took shape, the first was the rapid introduction of locomotives which could haul the heavier trains that the increasing summer traffic across the Island required. Standardisation became the second priority with the phasing out of obsolete and worn-out locomotives, and their replacement with a small number of locomotive types adapted to suit the needs of the Island lines.

Therefore, it was decided to settle on Adams O2 class 0-4-4 tank locomotives as the back-bone of the Island fleet, along with further *Terriers* to work the lighter trains, push-pull workings, and the Shide-Cement Mills chalk workings. Finally locomotives of the Stroudley E1 class 0-6-0 tanks were brought in to handle the heavy freight and other duties. In addition, there was an attempt after the war to introduce Billinton E4 0-6-2 tank locomotives, which proved abortive.

Above: A line up of the Southern's three 'standard' classes at Newport in the early days of British Railways. From left to right they are: O2 Class W25 *Godshill*; E1 class W4 *Wroxall*; and *Terrier* W13 *Carisbrooke*.
(Photographer Unknown)

Above: W4 *Bembridge* at Newport c1930 with a Freshwater line train. (Commercial Postcard)

Additional Terriers

W3 (W13) *Carisbrooke*

The first 'new' locomotives to arrive on the Island were the O2s, but three further *Terrier* locomotives were also transferred. First was former LBSCR No.77 *Wonersh*, which arrived in May 1927 as W3. Like the other Island *Terriers* W3 was equipped with an extended bunker, and also push-pull apparatus.

W3 was named *Carisbrooke*, and in 1932 was re-numbered W13 again to release numbers for the 'new' E1 class locos. W13 was withdrawn and returned to the mainland in May 1949. Renumbered 32677 it worked the Hayling Island branch until being withdrawn and scrapped in September 1959.

W4 (W14) *Bembridge*

Former LBSCR No.78 *Knowle* built in July 1880 arrived on the Island in May 1929 as W4 and named *Bembridge*. Again like W3 it was also renumbered to become W14 in April 1932.

However, W14's time on the Island was brief, departing again in May 1936. It then spent time on the Hayling Island branch and the KESR as No.2678. Following its absorption into British Railways stock it was numbered 32678. 1958 saw it back at Hayling Island, and then at Newhaven before it was withdrawn in November 1963. Happily it was preserved, and is now at the KESR.

W9 (2) *Fishbourne*

In May 1930 another *Terrier* arrived on the Island as a replacement for the original W9 that had been withdrawn in 1927. Formerly SR No. B650, W9 was built in December 1876 as LBSCR No.50 *Whitechapel*. Upon coming to the Island it was named *Fishbourne*, and fitted with an extended bunker. Again its time on the Island was truncated lasting only until May 1936.

After its return to the mainland it served in a number of places including Lancing Carriage Works and the Hayling Island branch where it was numbered 32650 until it was withdrawn in November 1963. The locomotive was then purchased by the Borough of Sutton & Cheam, and for many years was based on the KESR. It is now being overhauled on the Spa Railway at Tunbridge Wells.

Left: A very early colou photograph of W2 at Newport i grubby lined green livery in 1938.
(Photo: G.R.Whitelaw Collectio Copyright Colour-Rail/SR68

Medina and had formerly bee LBSCR No.136 *Brindisi* built i 1879. Like W2 and W3 it ha been overhauled at Eastleig prior to shipping, and had bee fitted with Westinghous brakes, as well as a Drummon pattern chimney. They wer painted in standard Souther passenger green.

W1 lasted in service until 1957 when reduced goods service led to its withdrawal.

E1 Tanks

Designed by William Stroudley as 0-6-0 goods tank locomotives, the first E1 entered service on the LBSCR in 1874. In total 79 of the class were built weighing in at 35 tons 19 cwt, with 4ft 6ins driving wheels and a tractive effort of 17,470lbs. They possessed good acceleration, and were also used for secondary passenger duties. One was rebuilt with a larger boiler in 1911, and ten as 0-6-2 tanks with the class designation of E1R. These were used extensively on the former LSWR lines in Devon and Cornwall.

Sadly only one member of the class has been preserved, No.110, which is currently being overhauled at the East Somerset Railway. The details of the Island E1s was as follows:

W1 *Medina* (2)

The first three E1s arrived together on the Island in July 1932 (see photo page 31 Volume One). W1 was named

Right: W3 *Ryde* at Newport on 10th April 1939.
(Photo: A. Duke Copyright Stephenson Locomotive Society)

W2 *Yarmouth*

W2 was previously ex-LBSCR No.152 *Hungary* buil in 1880. It was the first of the class to b withdrawn in 1956.

W3 *Ryde*

This was formerly ex-LBSCR No.154 *Madrid*, whicl served on the Island until June 1959, havin clocked up a total of 1,505,919 miles since originally entering service in 1881.

W4 Wroxall

W4 *Wroxall* was the final E1 to arrive on the Island in 1933. Originally it was ex-LBSCR No.131 *Gournay* built in 1878. With this locomotive Ryde Works solved a long-standing problem with the ride of all the E1 locomotives by re-balancing it.

The E1s were often used for hauling *The Tourist* through trains between Ventnor and Newport, with an O2 taking over for the leg to Freshwater. During their service they proved extremely capable and well suited to their work. W4 was the final member of the class in service and was withdrawn in October 1960.

Class E4 No.2510

This was very much the odd locomotive out as far as the Island was concerned. The E4s were designed by Robert Billinton for the LBSCR and first appeared in 1897. They were 0-6-2 tank locomotives weighing in at around 57 tons with a Tractive Effort of over 18,000 lbs, and were more powerful than any other locomotive on the Island.

When options were being considered for increasing the capacity of the Ryde-Ventnor line after the Second World War, the use of these locomotives was looked at to replace the O2s, possibly utilising push-pull working. Therefore, in February 1947 No.2510 arrived on the Island. Formerly ex-LBSCR No.510 *Twineham* built in 1900 it was to remain only until April 1949. Clearance problems were encountered during trials and the locomotive was not as economical as the O2s, which lead to the decision not to proceed with the idea.

SOUTHERN RAILWAY.   Ref: IN/25.

Office of Assistant for Isle of Wight,

NEWPORT, I. W.

29th July, 1932.

NOTICE TO DRIVERS & GUARDS AND OTHERS CONCERNED.

E.1 CLASS ENGINES, NOS. W.1, W.2 and W.3.

LOADS OF FREIGHT TRAINS.

The above engines may be permitted to work Freight trains on the following sections of line with certain loads as shown :-

Newport, Merstone and Sandown - 20 loaded Mineral wagons, and
                                1 Brake Van.
                    Vehicle limit for section 40 vehicles.

Medina Wharf and Newport - 30 loaded Mineral wagons, and
                           1 Brake Van.
                    Vehicle limit for section 45 vehicles.

For other loadings these engines should be classified in load class A. as shown on page 3 of the current Working Time Table.

late 40.

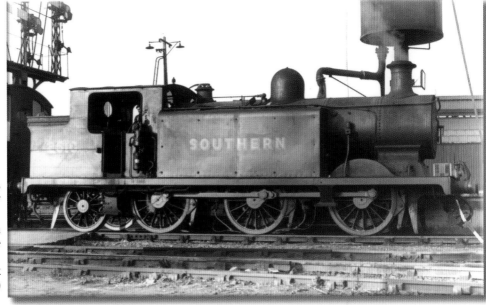

Right: As its stay on the Island was brief, photos of SR No.2510 are fairly rare. However, here it is with a train at Newport in June 1947.

(Photo: Copyright R.K. Blencowe)

The O2s

No other class of locomotive was more synonymous with the Island than the O2 0-4-4 tank locomotives, the first of which were imported to the Island by the Southern. Designed by William Adams in 1889 to work the London suburban services and branch line duties, eventually sixty members of the class were built, with the last emerging from Nine Elms Works in 1895.

They were powerful locomotives for their size, with rapid acceleration, and possessed a Tractive Effort of 17,245lbs. Originally weighing in at 44 tons 15.5 cwt, they were highly suited to more lightly engineered branch lines, such as those found on the Island.

W25 *Godshill* is seen here in its original form as LSWR No.190 at Nine Elms on 10th May 1902. Note the differences with W19 below fitted with a Drummond pattern chimney.
(Photo: LCGB/Ken Nunn Collection)

Recognising this in July 1903 the IWCR enquired if one could be purchased from the LSWR, but they could not agree a price. However, electrification of the London suburban network rendered a number of O2s redundant, and so when the SR was looking for new motive power for the Island they were considered ideal.

The first of these, ex-LSWR Nos.206 & 211, originally built in 1891 & 1892 respectively, were craned ashore at Ryde Pier Head in May 1923 and put into service. They were painted in LSWR livery, and still carried their LSWR numbers (see left). Later they were numbered W19 & W20.

Above: LSWR No.211, later W20 *Shanklin,* is seen on Ryde Pier.
(Photo: IWSR Collection)

Right: Former LSWR No.206 W19 is seen at Newport on 25th April 1926 in the first SR livery to be carried by the O2s on the Island. They did not start to be named until 1928 when W19 received the name *Osborne.* It was also one of the first O2s to be withdrawn in 1955.
(Photo: LCGB/Ken Nunn Collection)

O2 360 Degrees

Left: In total 23 O2s found their way to the Island the last being W36 in 1949, and over the years they went through a series of modifications. However, here we present a 'round-trip' around O2s in more or less their final form. Starting with W20 *Shanklin*, now in BR lined black livery, photographed at Ryde St John's Road from the coal stage by Dick Riley on 25th June 1957. To cure overheating in the cabs most of the O2s were fitted with vents on the cab roof, which is just visible in this photograph.
(Photo: R.C. Riley Copyright transporttreasury.co.uk)

Right: Following on from the photograph on the previous page ex-LSWR No.190 is seen at Newport in its Island guise as W25 *Godshill* in September 1953. Originally built in 1890 and coming to the Island in 1925, it was withdrawn in 1962. On the smokebox door is the shed-plate. The shed numbers were in early BR days 71E for Newport and 71F for Ryde, but in 1954 they became 70G and 70H respectively.
(Photo: J.H. Aston)

Left: W23 *Totland* was LSWR No.188 built in 1890 and imported to the Island in April 1925. It was to be one of the first withdrawn in August 1955 along with W34, and is seen here at Newport on 26th September 1951.
(Photo: G.F. Bloxam)

Right: Finally in this 360 degree tour is W28 *Ashey* seen departing bunker first from Ningwood on 16th September 1952. W28 was formerly LSWR No.186 built in 1890 and brought to the Island in March 1926. It was the first O2 locomotive to receive a nameplate in October 1928.
(Photo: G.F. Bloxam)

Boilers, Brakes, and Bunkers

The O2s received a number of modifications while they were on the Island. Some of them arrived with boilers designed by Dugald Drummond, which are recognisable by the safety valves mounted on top of the dome (see W27 below). Those fitted with Adams pattern boilers had smooth dome covers and separate safety valves and cover over the firebox (see W26 bottom of page). Locomotives fitted with Drummond boilers had them replaced while on the Island, but in the 1940s and 50s some Drummond boilers were re-used (see page 72), so it pays to observe the domes carefully.

Before coming to the Island all the O2s were fitted with Westinghouse air-braking equipment. This uses pressurised air to hold the brakes 'off' whereas the rest of the SR system on the mainland used vacuum brakes. The pump was attached to the side of the smokebox and a pressurised air tank added on top of the left-hand side tank. The final O2s to arrive on the Island, W35 and W36, imported by BR in 1949, also possessed air operated push-pull apparatus.

Finally, when they first arrived the O2s like W27 (left) had their original small coal bunker, which could only hold 1.5 tons of coal. Eventually all the O2s were fitted with an enlarged bunker holding up to 3.25 tons, starting with W26 Whitwell in September 1932, and seen below.

Original Coal Bunker with Coal Rails

Safety Valves Mounted on Top of Dome

Left: W27 Merstone at Newport.
(Photographer Unknown)

Brake Pipe   Lamp Iron   Westinghouse Pump   Dome Cover   Safety Valves & Cover   Air Reservoir   Enlarged Bunker

Headcode Disc

Steam Heating Pipe   Front Sandbox   Sanding Pipe   Rear Sandbox   Brake Rigging

(Photo: David J. Mitchell)

Liveries

Right: Over the years the O2s carried a variety of liveries, and space does not allow inclusion of them all here. When the first arrivals on the Island were repainted they sported the livery shown on W19 on page 124.

Later, after the locos were named, lined Southern olive green with nameplates mounted on the side tanks was the order of the day.

W14 *Fishbourne* ex-SR No.E178 built in 1889, and arriving on the Island in May 1936, is seen on the Down line at Brading Chalk Siding.

(Photo: IWSR Collection)

Left: Soon after the end of the war some locomotives were repainted in Malachite Green with *Sunshine* lettering. Here W18 *Ningwood* is seen at Ryde Shed on 29th March 1948.

W18, built in 1892, was SR No.E220, and came to the Island in May 1930, remaining in service until December 1965. Nos.W14-W18 were delivered to the Island after Nos.W19-W26, and given the numbers of the withdrawn IWR Beyer-Peacocks.

(Photo: J.H. Aston)

Right: This is a rare photograph of W34 *Newport*. Transported to the Island in May 1947 former SR No.E201, built in 1891, was outshopped by Eastleigh in LSWR Green with white and black lining and *Sunshine* lettering.

In September 1948 it was seen with the *Southern* logo painted out. Later that year it was painted in the livery which can be seen in the photograph on page 11. The locomotive only lasted in service until August 1955. This photograph was taken at Newport shed.

(Photo: Mike Morant Collection)

Left: W31 *Chale* came to the Island i[n] May 1927, having formerly been S[R] No.E180, built in 1890. It was the last o[f] the class to receive an enlarged bunke[r] in 1936, but one of the first to b[e] repainted in lined Malachite Green afte[r] the war. *Chale* was retained in servic[e] after the end of steam to help with th[e] electrification of the Ryde-Shanklin lin[e] and was not finally withdrawn unt[il] March 1967.

It is seen here at Newport in May 1949 with the *Southern* logo replaced wit[h] *British Railways* in hand-painte[d] lettering.

(Photo: W.H.G. Boo[n] Copyright Colour-Rail/BRS149[)]

Right: By the beginning of 1949 locomotives were beginning to be painted in lined black, a few of them appearing without a BR totem until it became available. Here W32 *Bonchurch,* the last O2 to remain in green, sports its new livery with the BR 'unicycling lion' totem at the water crane in the Newport platform at Sandown in October 1954.

(Photo: J.B. McCann Copyright Colour-Rail/BRS974)

Left: The final livery the O2'[s] carried is seen here as W1[6] *Ventnor* stands at Ventnor o[n] 28th August 1960, with th[e] totem applied to B[R] locomotives after 1956. W1[6] was one of the batch o[f] locomotives which arrived i[n] May 1936, having bee[n] originally built in 1892. It wa[s] to last in service until the en[d] of steam in December 1966.

(Photo: K.G. Carr Collection

Rolling Stock
Part One: Passenger Stock

Space does not permit the detailing of every item of rolling stock on the Island. However, these pages illustrate examples of the range of items that once graced the Island's rails, some of which still do on the Steam Railway.

The Isle of Wight Central Railway and its Constituents

The Isle of Wight Central inherited a 'hotch-potch' of coaches from its constituent companies, as illustrated by the train above. This photograph was taken on 11th May 1919, and shows IWCR No.7 departing Newport. The first carriage is an ex-R&NR five-compartment third of 1862. Next is IWCR No.12 an ex-LSWR single-compartment brake third, which survived into Southern Railways days, to be used as a mail van.

Following this comes an ex-Great East Railway (GER) five-compartment third of 1878 vintage. After which are two ex-LSWR four-compartment coaches, presumably one or both being composites, while the last vehicle is a former IW(NJ)R carriage rebuilt as a guard's van.

Among the vehicles the IWCR inherited were the 'stagecoach' coaches built in 1854 (seen below left), and bought by the R&NR from the LNWR for its opening. These were still in occasional use until around 1907.

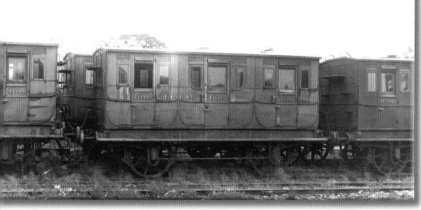

Somewhat ironically the IWCR came to possess the only bogie coaches on the Island before Grouping. The first two were built new for the Company in 1889. While the other two were the left-overs from their experimentation with railmotors.

Top: LCGB/Ken Nunn Collection
Bottom: Copyright National Railway Museum/SSPL

When railmotor No.1 was dismantled a second bogie was fitted to the coach portion to become IWCR No.52, and subsequently survived on the Island until 1949. The Midland Railway coach which was originally part of railmotor No.2, became IWCR No.7, and also survived into SR days. For sometime the two coaches ran on the Bembridge branch and can be seen right between St Helens and Bembridge with No.52 on the left.

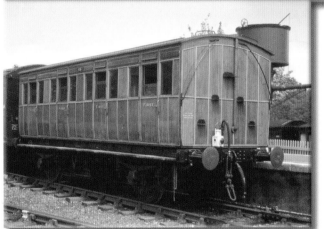

Isle of Wight Railway

In contrast to the IWCR the bulk of the carriage stock of the IWR came from three main sources. The first were those carriages supplied new to the IWR starting in 1864 by the the Railway Carriage Co. of Oldbury. They were four-wheeled carriages with first and second class compartments of varying layouts. Further batches totalling fourteen coaches were ordered up until 1882. They can be seen in the photos of IWR trains on pages 17, 29, and 78.

By the 1880s second-hand vehicles were being found. Two former Ryde Pier carriages were already on the

company books. In 1885 two six-wheel coaches and a four-wheel van originally supplied to the Golden Valley Railway were purchased. Then ten four wheel carriages formerly belonging to the North London Railway arrived in 1898. These became the first IWR coaches to be fitted with electric light using a Leitner lighting system. Happily one of these, No.46 (see left), a former four compartment first class coach withdrawn by the SR in 1926, has been restored by the IWSR from a grounded body.

The next arrivals in 1914 were eighteen eight wheel coaches (not mounted on bogies), built between 1879-84 for the Metropolitan Railway These became the mainstay of the IWR's carriage stock. Composite IWR No.22 (SR No.6344) is seen below at Whippingham sometime after its withdrawal in 1929.

Top & Middle: Photographer Unknown
Bottom: IWSR Collection

The Freshwater, Yarmouth and Newport Railway

When the FYNR started to run its own services in 1913 they had to find their own rolling stock. Some of this was in the form of two ex-LSWR five-compartment thirds, two ex-LSWR first/third composites, and an ex-C&NR brake third all purchased from the IWCR as part of the termination of their agreement. Four of these carriages (one of the composites is missing) can be seen in this picture with FYNR No.1 taken near Carisbrooke on 12th May 1919.

As this stock was fitted with air-brakes only FYNR No.1 was equipped to work them, FYNR No.2, as stated previously, only being equipped for vacuum braking. The seven carriages which No.2 was able to haul had been purchased from the Manchester South Junction and Altrincham Railway (MSJ&AR). They were all four-wheelers with four compartments. Three were thirds, two were first/third composites, one was a brake third, and the last a composite brake. All of them were to survive into SR ownership, and the two ex-FYNR composites Nos.4 & 6 (SR Nos.6358 & 6359), can be seen in the photograph to the left.

Right: When taken out of service the fate of many of the Island's carriages was to end up as grounded bodies, serving as houses (as with No.46), outhouses, chicken runs etc. Many of the Metropolitan Railway coaches ended up as beach huts at The Duver. Now heavily disguised with weatherboarding, their origins are only given away by the round-top doors.

Top: LCGB/Ken Nunn Collection
Middle: IWSR Collection

Southern Railway

Among the first items of rolling stock sent by the SR to the Island were nine ex-LSWR bogie coaches, built in the 1880s and 90s. These were transferred via Ryde Pier Head in July 1923. They were formed into three, three-coach sets and allocated to Newport for working the Cowes-Ryde and Cowes-Sandown services.

Next to be sent in 1924 were a batch of ex-LBSCR four-wheel coaches, that had originally been designed by Stroudley for use with the *Terriers* on the London suburban lines. These were formed into two, four-coach sets. Following on in 1925 came another twelve coaches. These were designed by Billinton, and were two feet longer than the Stroudley types with a higher roof profile. In addition, a first class saloon and horse box were transferred.

The SR wanted to introduce push-pull working to the Island and so the next imports in 1924 were two, two-coach sets of ex-London Chatham and Dover Railway (LCDR) stock. These had been converted from six-wheel carriages to four, and equipped to work as push-pull sets. There was a corridor connection between the coaches, and a small first class compartment. Numbered sets 483 and 484 they lasted in service until 1938.

Above: One of the LSWR sets is seen departing from Sandown for Newport behind ex-IWR W13 *Ryde*, directly behind the locomotive is one of the ex-IWCR ex-GER thirds. They were to survive on the Island until 1939.   (Photo: Copyright National Railway Museum/SSPL)

Above: Happily the two coaches which formed set 484 have been restored for service on the IWSR, and the driving end of brake third No.4112 can be seen at Smallbrook Junction in July 2008.

Left: One of the Billinton five-compartment thirds, No.2343, has again been restored from a grounded body and is seen at work on the IWSR.

Right: The ex-SECR railmotor coaches at Brading with ex-IWR W14 *Shanklin*.
(Photo: IWSR Collection)

The SR continued to pursue the introduction of push-pull working. In 1925 four bogie coaches arrived that had been converted from ex-SECR railmotors, and were intended to be used in two, two-coach push-pull sets on the Freshwater line with O2s W23 & W24. Trials did not prove satisfactory, and the idea was abandoned. For a time they were used on the Bembridge branch before leaving the Island in 1927. Eventually they were employed on the Westerham branch.

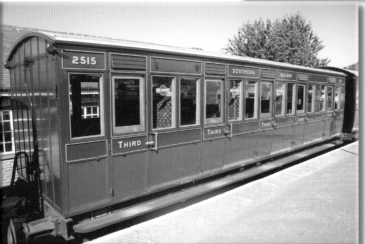

Above: A surviving example of the ex-LCDR four-wheel stock is third No.2515, seen here restored for use by the IWSR.

on the Ryde-Ventnor line, and so bogie coaches were imported. The first of these were again ex-LCDR coaches of 1897-8 vintage, which were in effect stretched versions of their four-wheelers. At 40 to 46ft in length they were shorter than average for such carriages, and so ideal for the restricted clearances on the Island.

In total 41 coaches were delivered starting in 1930. Most were employed on the Ryde-Ventnor Line, while they were also used for *The Tourist* through trains. Surviving the war, withdrawals began in 1948.

Next came the largest group of coaches transported to the Island in the 1920s which were further examples of former six-wheel LCDR stock converted to four-wheelers. In this case though, they were fitted for use in conventional trains.

Some 93 carriages were transferred: 45 thirds; 28 brake thirds; 16 composites and four luggage vans. Initially they were used on the Ryde-Ventnor service, first displacing the IWR four-wheelers and then the Metropolitan eight-wheelers.

By the 1930s there was again an urgent need for increased capacity particularly

Above: In August 1947 ex-LCDR bogie third No.2419 and an unidentified composite are seen at Newport.
(Photo: R.C. Riley Copyright transporttreasury.co.uk)

Left: An ex-LBSCR brake third, either No.4122 or 4123, is seen at Newport. (Photographer Unknown)

Further bogie coaches were still needed, and so ex-LBSCR stock totalling 63 coaches from a number of sources were dispatched to the Island between 1934 and 1947. Among the first were some brake thirds rebuilt in 1910 from six-wheel carriages, one of which is seen left top. Later groups had detail differences between them but the majority had been built new for the LBSCR around the time of the First World War.

In 1938 three ex-LBSCR coaches were sent to the Island to form push-pull set No.503. Two of the coaches had been built as a push-pull set in 1911, while the third had been built in 1921 as a trailer composite. They were to operate the Ventnor West branch for many years until the line's closure.

A second push-pull set No.505 from the same source was transferred to the Island in 1947, and was employed on the Bembridge branch as seen earlier in this volume. Both sets were withdrawn in 1954.

Middle: Ex-LBSCR third No.2415, pictured at Ventnor in 1960, was constructed in 1916 and came to the Island in 1936.
(Photo: K.G. Carr Collection)

Left: Push-pull set No.503 is seen at Merstone with W36 Carisbrooke. Note the additional fittings for push-pull working on the locomotive.
(Photographer Unknown)

The last group of coaches to be transferred to the Island were 52 ex-South Eastern & Chatham Railway (SECR) coaches built between 1910-11, which largely replaced the ex-LCDR bogie coaches. These arrived on the Island between 1947 and 1949, and so latterly were transported by British Railways.

One modification that was carried out was the provision of additional luggage space. This was achieved by the conversion of a number of brake composites to brake thirds, with over half the coach being available for luggage.

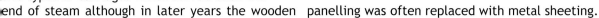

The SECR and LBSCR bogies were to be the two types of carriages which served until the end of steam although in later years the wooden panelling was often replaced with metal sheeting.

Other vehicles which counted amongst the passenger stock were those used for the transport of parcels and luggage. They included nine ex-LSWR bogie guards vans. Final transfers of stock to the Island took place under the auspices of BR in October 1950, and consisted of seven ex-SR passenger luggage vans.

Top: Ex-SECR brake third No.4145 in service on the IWSR in July 2008.

Middle: Compare the ex-LBSCR composite coach No.6350 on the right, with the ex-SECR one in the middle. Also note the assortment of signals. This scene was taken at the north end of the old Freshwater loop at Newport on 26th September 1962.
(Photo: P.F. Bloxam)

Right: Ex- LSWR bogie guards van No.1021 is pictured at Pier Head probably in the early 1950s. Having arrived on the Island in June 1937 it was withdrawn in October 1956. (Photographer Unknown)

Part Two: Goods Stock

Left: The IWCR did purchase some new wagons, and this manufacturer's photo shows IWCR wagon No.139 ready for delivery in 1889. Note the solid dumb buffers even on this new-built stock. At the time of the photograph standard IWCR goods livery was grey with white lettering, but this later became black with white lettering.
(Photo: Copyright HMRS Gloucester Railway Carriage & Wagon Collection)

The Isle of Wight Central Railway and its Constituents

The early railways on the Island were promoted primarily for the conveyance of passengers rather than goods, and indeed when it opened the C&NR only possessed four wagons, while the IW(NJ)R had only five 8-ton coal wagons. However, as the railways developed so did the amount of other traffic.

In the case of the R&NR they anticipated mineral traffic originating from Ashey Quarry, and there was also the transportation of coal across the Island. Therefore, by the time of the formation of the IWCR in 1887 some 148 wagons were recorded as being part of the Central's stock.

Most of these were open wagons for transport of coal and other minerals, but there was other traffic as well. Farming supplies had to be delivered, as well as parcels for merchants and shops. Livestock also needed to be conveyed, and so wagons had to be provided.

There was also provision for other specialist traffic such as two tank wagons that were purchased in 1898 for the transport of tar. Many of these acquisitions were second-hand, some new, and so the IWCR amassed an assortment of wagons. These had varying buffer and coupling heights, some were fitted with dumb buffers, and others sprung buffers. Dumb buffers were made illegal in 1913, but the IWCR was still using wagons with them up until Grouping in 1923.

Chalk traffic between Shide pit and Cement Mills was handled by rakes of private-owner wagons totalling 35 in number. Other private-owner vehicles were two timber trucks owned by A. Sharpe and Co. Eventually the IWCR was to hand over 317 goods wagons to the Southern.

Above: An interesting oddity. This brake van was one of two constructed by the IWCR workshop as 'goods brake and tranship van No.3' using the chassis from a Stroudley brake van. Coupled to it is ex-LSWR 10-ton road vehicle wagon No.60562 transferred to the Island in 1927. The date is c1950, and the location is probably Merstone.
(Photo: K.G. Carr Collection)

Above: A return to a previous photograph of Bembridge featured on page 90 gives a close look at three IWR wagons. The first two are 3-plank opens loaded with coal, and the one on the left is possibly one of the original wagons supplied new to the IWR by the Railway Carriage Co in 1864. Note that this one has sprung buffers, while the second one has dumb buffers. The third wagon is carrying timber and has shaped ends, it to has dumb buffers, and also carries the earlier form of IWR livery with smaller lettering. (Photo: IWSR Collection)

The Isle of Wight Railway

Unlike the IWCR the IWR's wagons came from two main sources. The first was the Railway Carriage Co. of Oldbury, which supplied many new wagons, particularly in the early days of the IWR. Later Ryde Works built or rebuilt wagons often with larger capacity. Here again the majority of the IWR wagons were used for the transport of coal and minerals, but wagons were also in use for transporting timber, road carriages etc. There were also covered vans and brake vans.

Buffers have already been mentioned, and six wagons with dumb buffers lasted in IWR service until 1923. However, another change that took place was over couplings, where hook and link couplings were replaced by

three-link couplings from 1893, the task being supposedly completed in 1905 when the older type became illegal. As with the IWCR the numbers of wagons increased through the years, from an initial 20 to 139 in 1889, until 221 were handed to the SR in 1923.

The Freshwater, Yarmouth and Newport Railway

Part of the settlement when the FYNR split with the IWCR was the purchase of 31 wagons by the

Right: One ex-IWR wagon which survived into BR ownership is Departmental wagon DS64351. It was a much altered 10-ton open built at Ryde Works and transferred to locomotive coal and ash duties in 1931. This view taken on 12th July 1964 is also interesting for the work taking place on wagons around it. To the right is No.27891 an ex-SR 8-plank sent to the Island in 1948. Behind the wagons is O2 W36 Carisbrooke, which had been withdrawn in June 1964. (Photographer Unknown)

Above: W1 *Medina* departs from Newport with the 2.55pm goods for Ryde St Johns Road on 24th September 1951. The majority of the wagons in the train are 5-plank wagons built to ex-LBSCR designs. 76 of these trucks were delivered new to the Island in 1924-6, being the last new rolling stock to arrive. The larger open that can be seen is probably an ex-SR 8-plank open, which were transferred to the Island by BR in 1948.

(Photo: G.F. Bloxam)

FYNR, comprising of 26 open wagons, 4 covered vans, and a brake van. This was one of the Stroudley designed ex-LBSCR vans the IWCR had purchased in 1902.

There were no further additions to this stock throughout the independent life of the FYNR. The only significant change being the conversion of five open wagons to cattle trucks by the addition of corrugated-iron roofs. One of these conversions is featured in the photograph on page 119.

The Southern Railway

When the Southern took over the Island lines, they realised that the goods stock was in as parlous a state as the rest of the infrastructure. Therefore, they embarked on a policy of replacement of the stock used for goods traffic, with what remained of the pre-Grouping stock being relegated to engineering and loco department use.

The bulk of the new stock imported were ex-LBSCR designs produced by Lancing Works. Here again open wagons dominated with 457 5-plank opens being provided out of a total of 618 trucks which arrived on the Island during the Southern's time.

Among the other types of wagons delivered were ballast wagons to assist with the permanent way renewals. Covered goods vans, and cattle trucks also featured, as well as bolster wagons and van trucks, along with 14 ex-LSWR brake vans.

By 1931 almost the entire Island goods stock had been provided by the Southern. After this the growth in goods haulage began to have an impact, particularly after the war. British Railways imported 88 SR-built 8-plank opens to replace 115 of the 5-plank stock, along with a further ex-LSWR brake van. These were to be the last goods vehicles to arrive on the Island for steam operations under BR.

Right: Ex-LBSCR 10-ton covered van DS46951. This was one of 35 built between 1920-23 with a 9ft 9ins wheelbase. It is seen here in September 1960. Later it was to be used as the match-van for the test running of the 'new' electric stock with W24 *Calbourne*, and a photo of it in this role can be seen on page 146.

(Photo: K.G. Carr Collection)

Below: Ex-LSWR brake van No.56055, one of 444 such vans built between 1887 and 1905. 56055 was originally built in 1894 as LSWR road van No.99. It was among of a group of 14 similar vans transferred to the Island in 1938, and is now preserved as part of the National Railway Museum Collection. This photograph was taken at Ventnor in 1962.

(Photo: H.W. Robinson Copyright J.F. Hyde, Steam Archive)

Left: Four of the ex-LSWR 10-ton brak[e] vans transferred to the Island were altere[d] in 1933 to provide a second, larger veranda as well as sanding equipment. Th[is] allowed them to be used on the fort[y] wagon coal trains which the E1s were no[w] permitted to haul on the Island. On[e] feature was the provision of Westinghouse brake pipe, thought to hav[e] been added to permit their use on th[e] Freshwater line mail train. Sadly n[o] examples of this type of van survived. Th[is] photograph of No.56047 was taken a[t] Ventnor on 5th September 1964.

(Photo: David J. Mitchel[l)]

Right: In 1948 British Railways supplied an extra brake van along with ex-SR 8-plank wagons. This was No.56058 a 18-ton van built in 1906 by the LSWR as a six-wheeler, but converted to a four-wheeler soon after. It was larger than the other vans on the Island with a wheelbase of 14ft, and a body length of 24ft. The photograph was taken in April 1962.

(Photo: Norris Forrest
Copyright transporttreasury.co.uk)

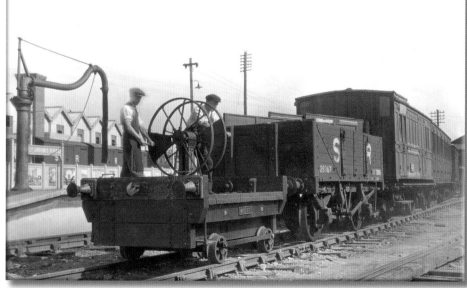

Left: One piece of equipmen[t] that was hard to categorise wa[s] *Midget*, built out of scrap part[s] at the behest of A.B. MacLeod i[n] 1930. It was used to shun[t] equipment around Ryde yard and was a 'hand-powere[d] tractor' capable of moving load[s] up to 20 tons. *Midget* wa[s] broken up in 1938.

It is seen here at St John's Roa[d] in 1930. Behind it is one of the 10-ton 5-plank open wagons and beyond that is tool va[n] No.438S. This was formerly IW[R] passenger guards van No.[4] supplied by the Railwa[y] Carriage Co. In 1864, and wa[s] condemned in 1930.

(Photo: Copyright Nationa[l] Railway Museum/SSPL[)]

Travelling Cranes

Right: The Isle of Wight Railway had two travelling cranes, both of which survived to the end of steam. The first was purchased from the Kirkstall Forge Co. in 1865 with a 2-ton capacity. After the end of steam services it was re-purchased by its makers for preservation. It is seen here with Railway Carriage Co. buffers and number 425S at Ryde St John's Road on 7th July 1957.
(Photo: Nick Nicolson Copyright transporttreasury.co.uk)

Left: The other IWR mobile crane was of 1876 vintage with a 10-ton capacity built by James Taylor of Birkenhead and numbered by the Southern 426S. It is seen here with match truck SR No.426SM (later DS3138), which was built from former IWR wagon No.107 at St Helens on 26th June 1950. Sadly this crane was not to survive after 1969.
(Photo: K.G. Carr Collection)

Right: A certain survivor is the ex-IWCR travelling crane, purchased from the Midland Railway in 1912 and rated at 5 tons, it was coupled with former IWCR wagon No.28 as a match truck. Seen here at Newport in Southern livery with the numbers 429S and 429SM, they have both survived to become part of the IWSR collection.

(Photo: IWSR Collection)

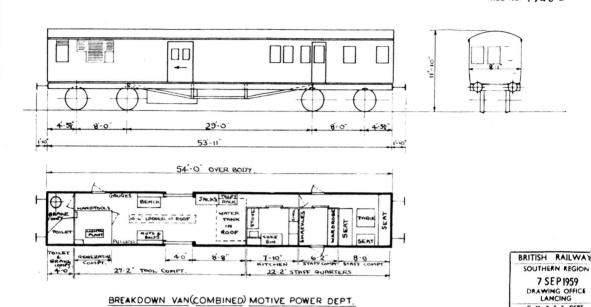

PAGE NO 1946

54'-0" OVER BODY

BREAKDOWN VAN (COMBINED) MOTIVE POWER DEPT.

BRITISH RAILWAY
SOUTHERN REGION
7 SEP 1959
DRAWING OFFICE
LANCING
C. M. & E. E. DEPT.
C. & W. SECTION

Below: The only addition which British Railways made to the engineering stock before the end of steam was the conversion of former LBSCR bogie composite saloon No.6986, which had been withdrawn in June 1956. In 1959 it was converted into a Breakdown Van, and renumbered DS70008. It was based at Ryde St John' Road as seen in the photograph below. Part of the plan are reproduced above.

(Photographer Unknown)

People

Of course railways are not just about locomotives or coaches or track etc. They are about people, the people who they serve, and the people who work for them. Throughout these two volumes drivers, firemen, signalmen etc have all featured. Here we have a selection of some of the other folk who make the railways work.

Right: Workers at the Newport Locomotive Works pictured with IWCR No.4 around 1900.
(Photo: IWSR Collection)

Left: Track-gangs are a vital part of the working railway community, there were 124 track workers on the Island in 1923, and here are a group posing as they align some newly laid & ballasted track.
Much of this work did not change over the years, and aside from the clothing this photograph could have been taken at any point up until the end of steam on the Island.
(Photo: IWSR Collection)

Right: Stationmasters and mistresses have featured in these volumes, but many people were employed at stations such as booking clerks and porters. Pictured are the station staff at Ventnor during SR days.
(Photo: IWSR Collection)

White House,
Ryde.

12. December 1927.

This is to certify that A. H. Butler joined the I.W Railway Co: about 1920, as a boy labourer – in the Ryde Loco: Shops- where he worked for about 2 years as Fitters and Boiler makers mate. He also assisted the Upholsterers. He then went to the Shed as a Cleaner for about 6 months - when he was promoted to Fireman on the Brading Harbour Branch. On my retirement in 1926 he was still firing – I found him a good steady worker - strong and a good time-keeper. Both his Father & Grandfather are old Railway Servants.

H.O.Tahourdin

SOUTHERN RAILWAY

General Strike — May, 1926

The Directors of the Southern Railway desire to place on record their grateful thanks to

Mr L C Turner

for valuable assistance rendered to the Company during the period of the recent General Strike.

The magnificent spirit displayed by all those who assisted the Company and the splendid work they accomplished, earned our admiration and enabled us to mitigate the hardships the travelling public would otherwise have had to suffer.

Their efforts are greatly appreciated by the Company.

WATERLOO STATION,
17th May, 1926.

H.A.Walker
General Manager.

Everard Baring
Chairman.

Sometimes we get glimpses of life on the railway through things other than pictures. For example, it is interesting to chart the career of A.H. Butler from boy labourer to fireman in the letter (left). More controversial are the events surrounding the General Strike of 1926, and of the volunteers who assisted in the operation of trains during it. The Southern Railway were, though, in no doubt that they were grateful to those who helped (above).

SPS (6/20)

SOUTHERN RAILWAY   No. 60312

The undersigned G Pierce (Mrs)
(name)

Female Painter   Ryde
(grade)   (station)

is AUTHORISED to be upon the Company's lines and premises in pursuit of his Railway Duties.

Issued by F. I. S. GILL   E. J. MISSENDEN,
                                 General Manager.

Signature of Holder   Per g H G Pierce

SOUTHERN RAILWAY.
To whom it may concern.

From Engineers Dept. To _____ My _____
      Bridge Section   7th.March. 19 46 Year
      Eastleigh.

Mrs G.Pierce.

The above named person was employed by the Southern Railway as a Female Painter for a period of three years, at Ryde Isle of Wight, during which time she was found to be satisfactory and honest worker.

Bridge Inspector.

It is undeniable that the ranks of railway-workers were very much male-dominated, with women only being employed to do clerical or administrative tasks. However, this changed during the two World Wars, when women found themselves undertaking a variety of roles. But when the men returned from fighting the expectation was that the women would step aside and allow them to take up their old jobs. This was probably the fate of Mrs G. Pierce, who having served as a female painter, was now seeking other employment in March 1946 (left & above).

The end of steam brought change for many people such as guards Percy Primmer, pictured left at Ryde Esplanade on 30th December 1966, and Roy Yule, photographed below the day after. For both of these men this was the end of an era, and things would never be the same again.

(Both Photos: Terry Hastings)

Left: But the railways would not exist without passengers, such as the crowds left waiting to board their train at Sandown on 22nd August 1964.   (Photo: IWSR Collection)

Below: For others though there were alternative attractions at railway stations such as the scene caught by Tony Bennett at Sandown station.

(Photo: A.E. Bennett
Copyright transporttreasury.co.uk)

runabout
cket covering the
st day one could travel
e entire Island network.

Electrification

Early Plans

Perhaps surprisingly, electrification of the entire Isle of Wight rail network was first discussed in 1899. A more serious investigation occurred in 1909 when a report prepared by William Upton Marshall suggested both the amalgamation and electrification of all the Island's railways. Marshall felt the Island's lines were woefully underutilised, with the average person only using them 20 times a year! Therefore, he advocated the formation of a single company, the Isle of Wight United Electric Railways Company.

This new company would then oversee the conversion of the entire system to a 'fast tramway service', using 10,000 Volt D.C. overhead equipment at a cost of some £310,000. New halts would be provided at places such as Yarbridge, Lake, Wellow and Northwood. He even proposed extensions from Ryde to Seaview; Newport to Osborne and East Cowes; and Freshwater to Totland. Sadly, or happily, depending on your point of view, the report was not acted on but the subject of electrification was to return just over fifty years later, and this time it was not destined

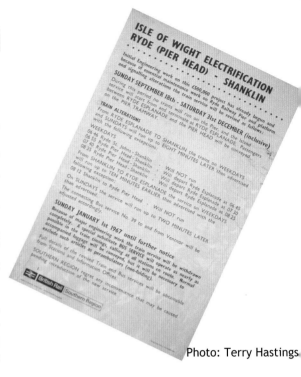

Photo: Terry Hastings

to remain simply a paper proposal.

A New Age

By the early 1960s only the lines between Ryde an Ventnor and Ryde and Cowes remained open, bu it was becoming clear that, without majo infrastructure investment closure was going to have t take place. One of the mai factors which affected th economics of the lines wa

Left: On a damp 4th Septembe 1966 W24 *Calbourne* is seen a Sandown conducting clearanc tests with the first of the ex-L carriages (S38S) to arrive on th Island. The van (No.46951 behind the loco had differen couplings mounted at each en to overcome the obvious heigh differences and couplin arrangements of the vehicles.
(Photo: A.E. Bennet
Copyrigh
transporttreasury.co.u

Right: On the last day of steam operation the LCGB special hauled by W14 *Fishbourne* and W24 *Calbourne* passes some of the new electric stock stored on the Down line south of St John's Road.
(Photographer Unknown)

that although overall the numbers of passengers using them were still significant, they were concentrated on certain days, particularly summer Saturdays.

On these days crowds of holiday makers would converge on Ryde Pier Head and the ferry services travelling to and from the Island. This meant that large numbers of trains were required for these particular days, which otherwise were underused the rest of the week.

Therefore, a number of alternatives were considered. The preferred option was the closure of the entire system, save possibly for a section from Ryde Pier Head to the Esplanade, or to St John's Road. This would act as a shuttle allowing the crowds using the ferries to be transferred to and from buses. However, there was strong opposition and so other ideas had to be looked at.

Another factor was the limited loading gauge on the Island, which precluded the use of ordinary mainland stock without major civil engineering particularly at Ryde in Esplanade Tunnel. This meant other solutions had to be found.

Options that were contemplated included the replacement of the O2s with BR standard 2-6-2 tank locomotives cut down to the Island loading gauge, possibly hauling trains of ex-London Underground (LT) stock. Dieselisation was also considered either using a fleet of nine diesel locomotives, or new-build multiple units.

Left: Ryde Pier Head station had been closed to allow work to be started on the electrification work in October 1966.
(Photo: Terry Hastings)

Left: The Down line from the Pier Head was also closed along with the line through Esplanade Tunnel to allow the track-bed to be raised. Here a train climbs the grade from the tunnel in December 1966.
(Photo: David J. Mitchell)

Below: Passenger numbers were still significant and so the 4-VEC and 3-TIS sets could be run as seven-coach trains known as 7-VECTIS. Here on 31st May 1983, the sets have been re-numbered classes 485 and 486 as two units headed by 485.041 start down from Esplanade to Shanklin.
(Photographer Unknown)

In the end it came down to the use of ex-Underground trains, either converted to diesel operation, or utilising 750V D.C. 3-rail electrification. Finally the decision was made to electrify the Ryde-Shanklin line, with the lines to Cowes and Ventnor being closed, the latter being on the basis of the additional cost of providing a sub-station at Wroxall. This was a move that was to prove very short-sighted, since it led to a substantial fall in income for the whole line. Half a million pounds was set aside for the project, and in 1966 work began.

Early in 1966 platform one at Ryde Pier Head was taken out of use and rebuilding started. In the September both the Down line through Esplanade Tunnel, and Ryde Pier Head station were closed, with trains terminating at Ryde Esplanade. This applied until the end of steam operations on the 31st December 1966, after which the line was completely closed to allow the work to be finished.

At Ryde Pier Head the station was reduced to two platforms, one of which was double-faced to allow for the rapid exit and entry of passengers. The

Left: Former 4-VEC set 485.043 heading towards Ryde pauses at Brading in March 1974. Interestingly Brading was still lit by gas lamps at this time.
(Photo: David J. Mitchell)

Shanklin a 400ft headshunt was kept in situ, as well as the loop-line, to permit two trains to be in the station at the same time. Signal boxes were retained at St John's Road, Brading, Sandown and Shanklin (open on summer Saturdays only), and were equipped with tokenless block instruments.

Stock

To operate the line 43 carriages of ex-LT 'Standard' stock built between 1923-34 were imported to the Island. These were formed into six four-car sets designated 4-VEC, and six three-car sets known as

track-bed was also raised to allow the floor of the 'new' carriages to line up with the platform edge. This was also carried out at the other stations, except at Esplanade where the platforms were lowered. In Esplanade Tunnel the track-bed was also lifted to improve the drainage.

Extensive changes were made at Ryde St John's Road where the former workshops were converted to house and service the new stock. Double track working to Smallbrook was made permanent, with the Smallbrook signal box being demolished. In addition substations were constructed at St John's Road, Rowborough, and Sandown.

At Brading the sidings were removed, while at Sandown the track into the former Newport-line platform road survived to serve two sidings. Beyond

Right: At Shanklin the old loop was used to permit the arrival of one train, while another stood in the old Up platform. This lasted until 1977 when the Up platform was taken out of use. Ex-3-TIS set 486.034 stands in the loop while 485.043 is at the Down platform in March 1974.
(Photo: David J. Mitchell)

Right: Ex-3-TIS set 485.044 branded for *Ryde Rail* is seen in the former Newport line platform at Sandown on 31st September 1990, probably awaiting scrapping.
(Photo: Ron Wyatt)

3-TIS units, with a spare car. The first car had been delivered in September 1966 and was used for clearance trails, being hauled between Ryde and Shanklin by W24 *Calbourne. Calbourne* was also retained in service following the end of steam along with W31 *Chale* to assist with the engineering work.

Meanwhile, further deliveries of the ex-LT stock continued until May 1967 when the last set entered service. By then the new electric service had been in operation for some weeks, having started on 20th March 1967.

For their new life on the Island the cars had been refitted with additional luggage space as well as new upholstery. Externally they were painted in the then new British Rail blue livery complete with the new BR logo flippantly referred to as the 'arrows of indecision'.

Operation

An hourly winter service was initially operated increasing to three trains an hour in summer, one terminating at Sandown, but on Saturdays five trains an hour departed from Ryde Pier Head. In January 1969 the pier tramway was taken out of service, and a pier shuttle was introduced, except for summer Saturdays and also Sundays, with the

Left: A new halt was formally opened at Lake on 9th July 1987 and here the 'opening' train is seen at the new facility with unit 485.045. The halt had actually come into use from May.
(Photo: K.G.Carr Collection)

Right: A change of guard in May 1990 at Ryde St John's Road.
(Photo: David J. Mitchell)

...train reversing at St John's Road.

In 1969 the sets were re-designated with 3-TIS becoming class 451 and the 4-VEC sets becoming class 452. Later, in 1973, the newly introduced TOPS system led to a further re-numbering with the 451's becoming class 486, and the former 452's class 485. A further change in operation occurred in 1973 when the crossover on the pier was taken out of use, and the pier was operated as two single lines.

From this time on there was a continued 'rationalisation' of services, rolling stock, and facilities. At Sandown the buildings and coverings on the former island platform were demolished. Then in 1977 the Up platform at Shanklin was taken out of use, and the signal box closed in July 1979.

On a more positive note, a new booking office was opened at Esplanade in 1978, and *Ryde Rail* branding was introduced to the line with logos being applied to the front and sides of the stock in 1985. However, it was not long before a new livery was to appear with the launch of Network South East in June 1986. A new halt was also opened

Left: In May 1990 unit 483.002 approaches St John's Road overbridge with a train from Pier Head.
(Photo: David J. Mitchell)

Right: Unit 483.004 departs from Ryde Esplanade for Pier Head. Note the two rear red tail-lights on the departing set, and also the modern 'road-style' speed-limit sign.
(Photographer Unknown)

at Lake in May 1987 at a cost of £80,000. This was something envisaged in the electrification plan of 1909, so only seventy-eight years late!

In August 1988 Network South East also announced that 'new' trains would be coming to the Island in the form of eight two-car ex-LT trains of 1938 vintage. This reflected the reduced usage of the system where now 16 carriages could suffice when 43 were once needed.

At Ryde St John's Road the workshops were re-arranged, with a raised road to facilitate the servicing of the under-floor equipment of the new stock. The first of the new units, designated class 483, started to arrive in July 1989, and by the end of May 1991 all the class 485 and 486 sets were withdrawn. By now the line had also been re-branded as *Island Line*, a name which has remained until the present date.

Further re-trenchment was to follow with the end of double-line working between Brading and Sandown in October 1988. This in turn led to the closure of Brading and Sandown signal boxes, with Ryde St John's Road now controlling the whole line. 1991 saw the opening of another new station on 21st July at Smallbrook Junction to provide an interchange with the newly extended Isle of Wight

Steam Railway.

Privatisation

By now there were questions once again over the whole future of the line. Government policy was now set on the Privatisation of the railways, and in 1994 the Ryde-Shanklin line became a 'shadow franchise' as part of this process.

Island Line was to be unique among the privatised franchises, in that the operator would also be responsible for the maintenance of the infrastructure under the supervision of Railtrack (and later Network Rail). There was even lobbying for the re-opening of the line to Ventnor.

Bus operator *Stagecoach* was eventually chosen to run the line. On 13th October 1996 the new management took charge. There was a new livery for stations, new initiatives in marketing, and costs were cut. However, losses continue to be made.

Some changes were startling. A new livery was unveiled in 2000 with a dinosaur theme. However, more recently all of the units have been repainted in London Transport red.

Left: On 10th February 2010 unit 483.007 heads down Ryde Pier towards Esplanade station. It is now possible to drive your car along the promenade pier to meet the ferry as witnessed by the car seen beyond the train. In the distance can be seen the mainland coast.

In 2005 the line became one of the first Community Rail partnerships, with the aim of helping to reduce the subsidy paid to the line. Meanwhile *Stagecoach* is set to remain the operator until 2017.

Several new proposals for the line have been made in recent years, including the conversion of the system to a tramway along with the re-opening of the lines to Ventnor, and to Newport from Sandown. An echo of the past was a proposal to link the system to the mainland via a tunnel under the Solent.

Questions do remain about the long term future of the line. Sadly one option, its conversion back to steam, seems unlikely as the cost of increasing the loading gauge in Esplanade Tunnel would be prohibitive. But maybe some radical thinking is necessary if the line is to survive for the future.

Right: 483.006 is seen later the same day at Shanklin station, which now has just a single platform in use, far removed from the days when crowds of arriving and departing passengers jostled to board or exit from the trains.

Diesel Locomotives

To help with the electrification programme, and also with ongoing engineering work and maintenance, British Rail sent a Class 05 Diesel Shunter to the Island in October 1966. D2554 was built by Hunslet in 1956 as an 0-6-0, with an eight-cylinder 204bhp engine. It had been assigned to the Eastern Region with the number 11140. After renumbering in the late 1950s D2554 continued to work at Parkeston Quay until its transfer to the Island. In order to permit it to fit the Island's loading gauge the cab roof was modified and reduced in height.

Above: D2544 is seen at Sandown on 26th May 1970.
(Photo: Copyright S.V. Blencowe)

It lasted in service on the Island's railways until 1984. During that period it was renumbered first 05001 under the TOPS system, then 97803. In 1984 it began to suffer from gearbox problems and so was replaced, being sold to the IWSR where it is still in service, although unable to work passenger trains due to the lack of air brakes.

D2554's replacement was Class 03 03079, which arrived on the Island in April 1984. This locomotive had been built at BR's works at Doncaster in 1960 as D2079, and spent much of its early life in the North-east before coming south. It was officially renumbered 97805 in 1984 but was never repainted, always being seen as 03079 on the Island. Like D2554 it was an 0-6-0 fitted with an eight-cylinder diesel engine generating 204 bhp, with drive being transmitted to the wheels by means of a jackshaft and coupling rods.

Later another member of the 03 Class arrived on the Island, 03179. Built as D2179 in 1962 at Swindon Works it spent much of its life before coming to the Island in and around Ipswich. Arriving in June 1988 it was resplendent in Network South East Livery, which it retained until its departure with 03079 in June 1998.

03079 was sold to the Derwent Valley Light Railway, while 03179 is still in service at Hornsey Depot in London, where it has been recently repainted in the livery of First Capital Connect. There is now no resident diesel locomotive on the Ryde-Shanklin line.

Left: 03079 faces different weather conditions to those it was used to on the Isle of Wight, as it provides the Motive Power for the Derwent Valley Light Railway's Santa Special on 22nd December 2009.
(Photo: Jonathan Stockwell)

The Ryde Pier Tramway

Motor car No.1 heads down towards Esplanade from Pier Head with trailer No.8 in tow on 5th September 1964. No.1 was one of two initially petrol-driven cars supplied to the Southern by Drewry in 1927, ironically the same year the ex-FYNR Drewry railcar was scrapped. By the time of this photo a diesel engine had been fitted to No.1.
(Photo: David J. Mitchell)

Ryde Pier has a special significance in that it is claimed to be the first pier in Britain. The first part of the pier was opened in July 1814 by the Ryde Pier Company (RPC) to allow passengers to board and disembark from vessels other than at high tide. In April 1825 a regular summer paddle steamer service began between Portsmouth and Ryde, operated by the Portsmouth and Ryde Steam Packet Company (P&RSPC), which became year-round in 1827.

By 1833 the pier had been extended to 2,250ft, and in October 1842 a pier head was added which could handle up to four vessels at a time. The pier was also being used as a promenade for people to walk 'over the sea'. Band concerts began in 1841, with a refreshment stand opening in 1845, and a W.H. Smith bookstall in 1856. Four years later the pier head was also extended.

The Idea Of A Tramway

The issue of how passengers and their luggage could easily be conveyed from one end of the pier to the other was now being seriously considered. At that time those who did not wish to walk had the option of being transported in bath chairs, while numerous 'porters' jostled for the opportunity to carry passengers' luggage on their trolleys down the pier to waiting carriages. In order to sort out this chaotic state of affairs it was decided to build a tramway.

In September 1861 a contract was let for the construction of a tramway on what was effectively a second pier built along the eastern side of the promenade pier. By July 1863 one line of the tramway was available to allow baggage to be transported in horse-drawn luggage vans.

Left: The tramway has bee[n] extended to St John's Roa[d] by the time this photograp[h] was taken, as the east line on the left is advertised a[s] *To the I.W. Railway*, whi[le] the west line on the right [is] advertised as going *To Ryd[e] Pier Gates*. Two of th[e] double-deck cars can b[e] seen on the left, with th[e] *Grapes* car behind. In th[e] siding in the lef[t] background, two mor[e] double-deck cars can b[e] seen.

(Photo: IWSR Collection[)]

However, the issue of what motive power would be used in the long-term was still under discussion.

Eventually the decision was made to employ steam-power and in November 1863 an approach was made to Manning Wardle & Co. to supply a locomotive. This duly arrived in March 1864, but after trial runs it was established that the pier structure was not strong enough for the weight of the locomotive. It was returned to the manufacturer and subsequently sold to the Northfleet Coal and Ballast Co. in Kent. Therefore, the decision was made to employ horse-power, and a passenger service began on 29th August 1864.

By now both tramway tracks were available for us[e] and so a second carriage was delivered in 1865[.] This was placed on the east running track, with [a] third carriage delivered in 1869. At the pier head [a] small turntable gave access to a number of siding[s] including a stable. Meanwhile at the pier gates [a] triangular platform served both lines, the easter[n] line curving away with a run-round loop, and [a] small carriage house as well as a siding along th[e] quay. The new tramway made travel along the pie[r] much easier, but there was still the need to fin[d] another means of conveyance to St John's Road and the terminus of the newly opened IWR fo[r] passengers travelling beyond Ryde.

Through to St John's Road Station

However, by this time a second pier, the Victoria[,] had been constructed by a rival company, the Isl[e] of Wight Ferry Company (IWFC). They had als[o] built docks and a tidal basin to the east of Ryd[e] Pier, much to the consternation of many of the townsfolk, who did not wish to see a commercia[l] port established. A ferry service from the Victori[a] Pier to Stokes Bay had also begun in 1863.

There then followed a period of intense competition between the two operations, not leas[t] in seeking to connect their undertakings with the IWR at St John's Road. In the end the IWFC wen[t] bankrupt in 1865 with the RPC acquiring the Victoria Pier and docks.

Up until this point one of the principal obstacles t[o] a connection between the IWR and the pier was the

Looking along the pier from Pier Gates from one of the trailer cars post electrification. (Commercial Postcard)

This photograph taken in 1927 shows the *Pollard* and *Grapes* cars running on the tramway, while one of the recently arrived O2s steams in the station behind. The fine bracket signal is also still in place.　　　(Photo: IWSR Collection)

Ryde Commissioners, who were the local government body for the town. They particularly objected to the concept of any railway or tramway dividing the town from the sea-front, and spoiling the view. However, in 1868 Ryde became a municipal borough, and the new Ryde Corporation proved far more amenable to the idea of a connection being made.

An initial extension of the tramway to Ryde Castle opened in January 1870, and in the November work began on an extension to St John's Road. This took an interesting route along the sea-front, before turning away from the sea across The Esplanade and through an arch constructed in the ground-floor of Holywell House.

From here the line passed across marshland, where a new channel for Monkton Mead Brook was dug, with the tramway on the western bank. At St John's Road a wooden island platform was built for the tramway, which was opened for traffic on 7th August 1871.

With the opening of the new section the RPC acquired six new double-deck carriages, still horse-drawn. Five were constructed by Starbuck & Co., while the sixth was built locally for the conveyance of first class passengers and VIPs, and became known as the *Grapes* carriage because of its ornate decoration.

Horse-drawn operation was though proving slow and costly, therefore, once again thoughts turned to the use of steam power on the line. A steam tram loco was acquired on loan from Merryweather in 1876, and trials proved successful. However, the Corporation refused permission for its use on the line to St John's Road, and so it was returned to the manufacturer. Eventually it went to the National Rifle Association at Wimbledon. By 1878 281,797 passengers were using the tramway annually, but now plans were being made to build the new Joint Line described earlier.

A Pier Tramway Once More

With the construction of the Joint Line under way, through services on the tramway ceased in 1880. The line being cut back to the route between Pier Head and Pier Gates. In 1881 there was yet another attempt to find alterative motive power for the

Left: Motor car No.1 and Trailer No.3 on the east line c1930.
(Photographer Unknown)

which left it short of money to effect necessary repairs to the pier and tramway, both of which were in a poor state. As a consequence of this the east running line was removed in 1883/4, and when the locomotive boilers were in need of repair horse-haulage was resumed.

However, the outcome of a court case between the RPC and the mainland companies revived the RPC's fortunes. In essence, part of the agreement between the RPC and the mainland companies for the construction of the new line to the Pier Head was that the companies had to pay a toll of 3d (1.5p) to the RPC for every passenger that travelled by train along the line. This the railway companies had only been charging on passengers booked to and from stations in Ryde. In 1885 the RPC won the case that the toll should apply to all passengers, and the judgement included the payment of arrears totalling over £6,500.

line when two new locomotives, rebuilt from tramway cars by Mr Bradley of Glensmore Works at Kidderminster, arrived on the line. These were originally designed to be worked by gas, but in trials the first locomotive consumed three times the amount of gas that was estimated. So they were converted to burn coke. However, their weight caused problems to the permanent way, and pier structure.

The short life of the extension meant that the RPC had not been able to recoup its capital outlay,

The Pier Head terminus was rebuilt in the 1890s and the roof was used by the Yacht Club for events, and as an observation platform. Here motor car No.1 waits with trailer No.8 on 27th February 1965.
(Photo: David J. Mitchell)

With this new financial windfall the Company pressed ahead with a decision to electrify the line. A contract was let with Siemens Bros and Co. for the supply and installation of the necessary infrastructure. The first experimental trip was made with the new equipment on 6th March 1886, and passenger services started on 4th April. Electricity was produced by a generator at the landward end of the pier and supplied to the power cars, which were converted from two of the Starbuck cars, by means of a conductor rail some eighteen inches above the level of the running rails, and to the side. Known as the Ryde Pier Electric Railway it was the first standard gauge electric passenger tramway in England.

In 1890 the second track was re-instated, but could not be fully worked until a new generator was installed in 1891. In 1892 the tramway carried 236,269 passengers. That year as well a new six-wheel motor car capable of carrying up to 100 people was delivered from the Lancaster Carriage and Wagon Co., but its long wheelbase produced excessive wear. So in 1907 it was converted into two four-wheel vehicles. Meantime re-construction of the tramway pier was authorised at a cost of £14,655, which was completed by 1899.

As part of the tramway pier reconstruction a new station was built at the pier head with an ornate overall roof. The top of this was used as an observation platform by members of the Royal Victoria Yacht Club, sometimes with a temporary awning.

During the first years of the 20th Century little seemed to change on the tramway. One addition came in 1911 when a new motor car was supplied by Pollard. Victoria Pier had been bought in 1916 by Ryde Corporation, but it had to be demolished when damaged in gales shortly after.

The outbreak of the First World War severely affected the Pier Company's income, as it did not benefit from the compensation scheme which helped the railways. As a result there was a gradual accumulation of neglected maintenance, that had become significant by the end of the war.

But the tramway was still carrying large numbers of passengers, 250,450 in 1921, rising to 331,284 in 1923. In 1924 the pier and tramway were sold to the Southern Railway for £84,000, with Ryde Corporation leasing the promenade pier and pavilion.

Special events added to the Pier Company's income. Tiered seating was provided on the pier head for people to view the fleet review in connection with Queen Victoria's Golden Jubilee in 1887, and crowds converged on the pier once again for a similar event to mark her Diamond Jubilee in 1897. The addition of a new pavilion on the pier head in 1895 also produced an extra source of revenue.

Right: A crowded car No.2 with trailer No.7 and luggage trolley No.9 in use on Ryde Pier on 5th September 1964.
(Photo: David J. Mitchell)

Under the Southern

At this point the tramway's electrical equipment was in a very poor state of repair, therefore a decision had to be made about the line's future. So in 1927 the Southern ordered two four-wheel petrol railcars from Drewry and Co, at a cost of £1,045 each. These were fitted with Baguley 26hp four-cylinder petrol engines, and electric operation was abandoned in October that year.

Trailer No.3 and the *Grapes* car, No.4, were initially partnered with the railcars, having been painted in SR livery, but in 1936 and 37 they were replaced with purpose-built trailers from Eastleigh Works, numbered 7 and 8. No.4, having been involved in an accident in 1935, was replaced first. It was eventually reconstructed as a single-deck horse-drawn carriage, and presented to the Hull Transport Museum. No.3 did not fair as well and was broken up. Happily the Pollard-built car also survived following its withdrawal in 1927, eventually going on display at the Isle of Wight Bus Museum.

The petrol-driven railcars were to serve the Tramway until it closed, save for the replacement of their engines, first in 1946/9, and then in 1959/60, on the last occasion with six-cylinder Perkins diesel units. There was one more addition to the stock when a luggage trolley, No.9, was added to the fleet as a replacement in 1939.

During the Second World War there was a severe reduction in services, but following the war passenger numbers quickly built up again, with the Portsmouth ferries carrying over three million people every year during the 1950s. By this point the tramway was operated by British Railways, but save for maintenance little work was done on it. However, the railcars were often filled to capacity moving an estimated 1,500 people an hour from one end of the pier to the other.

With the completion of the electrification programme in 1967 it was soon proposed that the tramway would close. The last trams ran on 26th January 1969, the railcars being draped, somewhat inappropriately, with flags bearing the emblem of British Rail.

In 1971 the rails were lifted, and now there is only the pier structure to be seen. Railcar No.2's chassis has survived, and is now at Havenstreet awaiting restoration. Today cars are allowed along the promenade pier to drop-off and collect passengers from the ferries, vying with those still trying to enjoy a 'walk over the water'.

Right: There is a sombre air among the passengers of the last tram along the pier on the night of 26th January 1969.

(Photo: Terry Hastings)

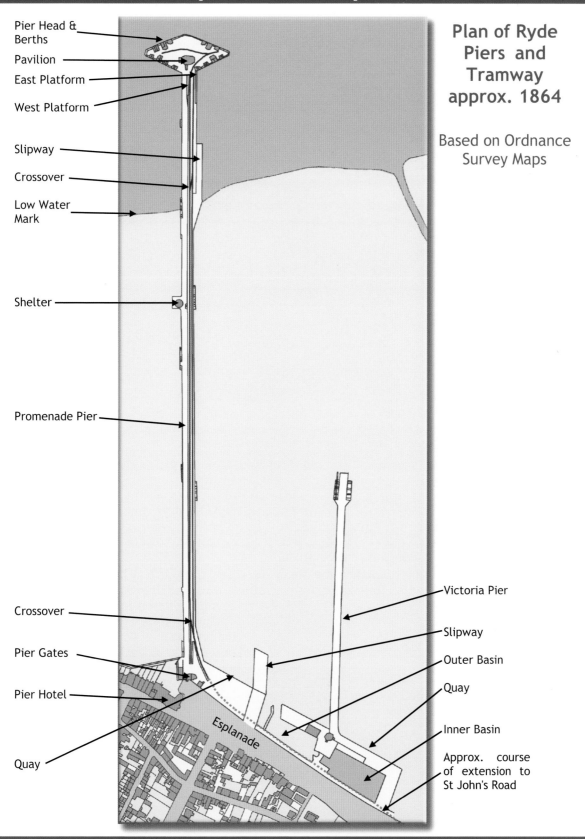

Pier Head &
Berths

Pavilion

East Platform

West Platform

Slipway

Crossover

Low Water
Mark

Shelter

Promenade Pier

Crossover

Pier Gates

Pier Hotel

Quay

Plan of Ryde
Piers and
Tramway
approx. 1864

Based on Ordnance
Survey Maps

Victoria Pier

Slipway

Outer Basin

Quay

Inner Basin

Approx. course
of extension to
St John's Road

Esplanade

The Isle of Wight Steam Railway

Above: Preservation at its best with an authentic ex-SR push-pull train consisting of ex-FYNR No.2 later SR No.8 *Freshwater* with the restored set No.484 which operated on the Ventnor West branch for many years. Below the same photo rendered in black and white brings a reminder of days past. (Photo: Alan Doe

Early Preservation

It has to be said that the concept of preserving the Island's railways' past is not new. One of the principal figures who sought to ensure the survival of at least some equipment from them was A.B. MacLeod. He had served as Assistant for the Isle of Wight from 1930-1934 having arrived on the Island in 1928, but he maintained a life-long interest in the lines.

Along with the Railway Correspondence and Trave Society (RCTS), MacLeod was responsible fo efforts to preserve W13 *Ryde* when it wa withdrawn in 1932. Sadly these efforts failed and having been transported to Eastleigh in 1934 (see photo page 115), W13 was cut up in 1940.

However, this was only one aspect of preservation efforts which led to a significant number of railway artefacts being saved for prosperity, including by MacLeod himself. The Island's isolation and limited loading gauge also contributed to it becoming a *de facto* living railway museum as every locomotive and carriage design operating on the lines until the end of steam was from the pre-grouping period.

Therefore, it is not surprising that with the survival of steam on the Island right into the start of the preservation era, there would be moves to save some aspects of the lines fo future generations. Indeed one anonymou but far-sighted civil servant in 1965 even suggested that the entire surviving network should be preserved as a working steam railway under British Rail. He recognised that this could prove attractive to the public as well as enthusiasts. If only he had been listened to!

The Wight Locomotive Society

In the mid 1960s, with the closure of the Island's railways very much on the cards, there was great interest from rail enthusiasts from all over the country and beyond. Many made their way to the Island either as individuals or as part of organised railtours to pay their respects as the end of steam approached. There were also schemes to preserve some of the locos and coaches, but most of these involved transporting them to the mainland to become part of preservation efforts there. Seemingly there was no real move to establish a preserved railway on the Island; in part this was because of the apparent prospect of the line from Ryde to Cowes being re-opened by the *Sadler-Vectrail* partnership, but, as was noted in Volume One, this did not happen.

In the meantime one group of individuals did get together, and were ultimately successful in their efforts to preserve at least something of the Island Railways' past. This was the Wight Locomotive Society (WLS), which had been formed in 1966 with

WIGHT LOCOMOTIVE SOCIETY
The Isle of Wight Steam Railway Centre
HAVEN STREET STATION, Nr. RYDE

WIGHT STEAM!

The Wight Locomotive Society has created a new and unique attraction for the Island in the form of a preserved steam railway, established so that both holidaymakers and local residents alike may continue to sample the delights of a vintage train in action.

YOU TOO CAN ASSIST IN THIS PROJECT BY JOINING THE SOCIETY — COMPLETE THIS MEMBERSHIP FORM AND SEND WITH REMITTANCE — TODAY! TO THE MEMBERSHIP SECRETARY, WLS, 58 HUNNYHILL, NEWPORT, I.W.

How You Can Help

Our Society has been built up entirely by VOLUNTEER EFFORT and PUBLIC SUBSCRIPTION. We ask you to help our work forward by making a donation or by becoming a member.

Write TODAY (enclosing S.A.E) to :
THE W.L.S. MEMBERSHIP SECRETARY
58 HUNNYHILL, NEWPORT, ISLE OF WIGHT

a target of raising £1,500 to save one O2 locomotive, and some coaches. This was with a view to possibly running them on the *Vectrail* line.

Initially their efforts met with very limited success. However, interest in the lines generated by the events organised to mark the end of steam, and the involvement of enthusiasts such as Sir Peter Allen and David Shepherd, ultimately led them to be able to purchase W24 *Calbourne*, for £900, and five coaches.

Left: *Calbourne* was overhauled in the open at Newport by a team of volunteers ready for service on the proposed Steam Railway.
(Photo: Terry Hastings)

Left: Five-compartment ex-LBSCR brake third No.4168 being restored at Newport in 1967.

(Photo: Terry Hastings)

The Steam Railway

The WLS had negotiated with the County Council to lease the line between Havenstreet and Wootton as a base of operations, so rapidly organised the transfer of the stock there. On 24th January a series of trains departed from Newport to Havenstreet to transport stock and salvaged items to their new home.

It has to be said that while the manner of departure was somewhat precipitate. In fact the railway authorities had done much to help the group in terms of allowing them to purchase a large number of items at virtually scrap prices. Therefore, there was a large amount of material to be transported, and it was not until 8.50pm that the last vehicle left Newport station.

A sixth coach was also donated when a plan to move it to Canada failed.

All these were stored at Newport station, while negotiations about the future of the Ryde-Cowes line continued. During this time other vehicles were added to the collection, including the former No.2 Ryde Pier car when the Pier Tramway closed in 1969.

However, when the *Vectrail* scheme failed, the line was handed over to the scrap-merchants, and the Society was given notice on 20th January 1971 to vacate the site at Newport by the 25th January. Therefore, yet another remarkable effort took place to save their collection once more.

At Havenstreet it was not long before a passenger operation began. A push-pull shuttle operated on Easter Monday 12th April 1971 over a mile length of the track, and in the May a seasonal service was started. In 1972 a limited company was formally incorporated, and the Isle of Wight Steam Railway was born.

Right: The first public steaming of *Calbourne* took place in Newport yard in November 1970.

(Photo: Terry Hastings)

Left: Part of Terry Hastings' copy of the Working Timetable for the movement of stock from Newport to Havenstreet on 24th January 1971.

WIGHT LOCOMOTIVE SOCIETY

SPECIAL NOTICE NO. 2 | REMOVAL OF STOCK, NEWPORT TO HAVEN STREET SUN. 24TH JANUARY

1. COMPLETE WORKING TIME TABLE

UP Train No.	1	2		5	7	8	10	11
	Rail Motor Car	Passgr.		Passgr.	Goods	Rail Motor Car	Goods	Rail Motor Car
To convey Staff or Ticket	Ticket	Staff		Staff	Staff Tkt.if Q runs	Staff	Ticket	Staff
NEWPORT dep	10.00UL A	10.40DL		12.15DL	13.45UL	15Q00UL B	15Q30UL	16Q40UL B
Whippingham	A	10/48		12/23	14/00	B	15/45	B
Wootton	A	10/53		12/27	14/06 C	B	15/51 C	B
HAVEN STREET arr	10.20DL	11D00UL		12D35UL	14.20UL	15Q20	16.05DL	17Q00
DOWN Train No.		3	4	6		9		
		Rail Motor Car	Engine	Engine		Engine & Van		
To convey Staff or Ticket		Ticket	Staff	Staff		Staff		
HAVEN STREET dep		11.10DL	11J40UL	12J50UL		14Q30UL		
Wootton			AB					
Whippingham			AB					
			AB					
NEWPORT arr		11E30UL	12J00DL	13J10UL		14Q50UL		

A = Set Down Crossing Keepers as necessary at Halberry House, Mews Lane, Packsfield.
B = Pick up   "   "   "   "   "   "
C = Stop at Up Distant Signal to pin down Wagon Brakes.
D = Run to Up Loop, Engine run round and propel to Single Line, Ashey side of Station.
E = Run to Up Loop, thence to Third Road and berth.
Q = Runs if required.
DL= Down Loop.
UL= Up Loop.

10.40 Newport to Havenstreet formed Carriages Nos. 2416, 6349, 4168.
12.15 Newport to Havenstreet formed Carriages Nos. 4145, 6375, 4149.

Above: W24 is prepared for a busy day moving stock from Newport to Havenstreet on 24th January 1971. Water had to be pumped into its tanks as the water towers at Newport had been disconnected by this time.

(Photo: Terry Hastings)

Early Days

Like the history of many early preservation efforts, the initial days of the IWSR were very much ones of making the best of what they had. But there were surprising opportunities as well, such as the one which led to the arrival of a second steam locomotive to Havenstreet in June 1971. *Invincible*, an 0-4-0 saddle tank built by Hawthorn Leslie, had operated on the Royal Aircraft Establishment's line at Farnborough, and came initially on loan to the Railway. It was to prove invaluable in those early days. 1972 saw the arrival of an 0-6-0 Andrew Barclay-built tank locomotive of 1918 vintage called *Ajax*. However, it was not destined to enter service until 2005.

Meanwhile other work was underway. At Havenstreet one of the original water towers from Newport station was erected along with a coaling stage. At the site of the original Wootton station work was under way to re-open the platform, and widen the trackbed beyond the station to allow a run-round loop to be built. Sadly a series of landslips led to the abandonment of the scheme in 1974, and the site was filled in. Instead a new station was created to the east of the road bridge.

On a much happier note 1973 saw the return to the Island of another original Isle of Wight locomotive,

when W11 *Newport* arrived back on 27th January from Pwllheli. The society also began to rescue some of the grounded coach bodies which were lying around the Island, and being used for various purposes.

STEAM TRAINS at HAVENSTREET STATION

Open June to September and Bank holidays

Station open from 10 am daily
In Steam every Sunday

A No 3 bus from Ryde or Newport takes you straight there

Car park

Refreshments available

Left: W11 *Newport* arrives back on the Island on 27th January 1973.

(Photo: Terry Hastings)

The centenary of the opening of the original Ryde and Newport Railway occurred in 1975, and so to celebrate this it was decided to hold a Steam Show over the August Bank Holiday weekend. This event was notable for several reasons, it was the first of the regular events which continue up to the time of writing. It also marked the unveiling of a cosmetically restored W11 *Newport* in IWCR livery, and was the occasion of the author's first encounter with the railway.

Work had also continued on the new station at Wootton, and a run-round loop came into use in August 1977. On 25th June 1979 another ex-IOW locomotive returned in the shape of W8 *Freshwater* after her duties as a pub sign. She proved to be in much better condition than W11, and returned to steam in September 1980.

Right: To celebrate the centenary of the opening of the R&NR in 1975 the IWSR organised the first of their Steam Shows over the August Bank Holiday Week-end. *Invincible* was fitted out with a headboard for the occasion reminiscent of the one carried by IWCR No.6 for the opening of the NG&SLR in 1897.

Consolidation

The 1980s saw continued developments on the railway. New workshops came into use in 1981, and a brick-built refreshment room opened next to the original station building at Havenstreet in September 1982. In 1983 the railway acquired the former retort house of the old gasworks and further land around the station has been bought as

Left: As part of the centenary celebrations W11 was unveiled cosmetically restored in IWCR livery. Happily it was to eventually return to steam in 1989.

Extension

It had always been one of the railway's ambitions to extend the line to Smallbrook to connect with the line from Ryde to Shanklin. During the 1980s discussions began to make this a reality. This led to an agreement with Network South East, which by now was responsible for the operation of the Ryde-Shanklin line, for an interchange station to be built. The railway also benefited by the recovery of the track parts made redundant by the singling of the Brading to Sandown section, as well as from the line between Alton and Farnham.

The first length of track on the new extension was laid on 25th August 1989, and, after much effort by volunteers and contractors, the line was ready for use on 20th July 1991. It was therefore with great celebrations that W24 pulled the inaugural train into the new station. That year over 100,000

the years have passed.

Former IWR four-wheel coach No.46 returned to service after an award-winning restoration, while the railway won another award for the 'new' Wootton station which came into use in August 1986.

The end of the decade was also marked by celebrations for the centenary of the opening of the FYNR in 1889, with W8 being repainted in its former FYNR livery and re-numbered No.2. In August the line's other *Terrier*, W11 *Newport*, also returned to service. There was indeed much to be optimistic about, for by then work was about to begin on the railway's most ambitious project, the restoration of the line to Smallbrook.

Right: Another *Terrier* returned to the Island when former ex-FYNR No.2 later SR W2 and then W8 *Freshwater* was unloaded at Havenstreet on 25th June 1979.
(Photo: Terry Hastings)

Left: This building started life as the signal box at the FYNR's Newport station, before being moved to Freshwater. After the closure of that line it then served as a bus shelter, before the IWSR rescued it and put it back into service at Wootton. It is seen here in July 2008.

passenger journeys were made on the line, a record at that time, and the new link with *Island Line* proved to be beneficial to both sides.

To the Millennium

The new extension and increasing passenger numbers meant that there was a need for new, larger locomotives. Therefore, the arrival of Hunslet Austerity *Royal Engineer* in February 1992 on long term loan from the Royal Corps of Transport Museum Trust, along with a Barclay 0-4-0 Diesel was very welcome, particularly as *Calbourne* required major work which would keep it out of action until 1995.

The mid-1990s offered tough challenges for the railway in difficult economic circumstances, but there were many positives. On 2nd May 1993 Ashey station was re-

opened using the short platform that had been brought into use in 1961. Another major landmark came in July 1993 when ex-LCDR composite coach No.6369 was reunited with its previous running-mate driving brake third No.4112 to form push-pull set No.484. This set operated on the Ventnor West branch for many years, and so another authentic part of the Island's railways' past was recreated.

Another revival occurred on Sunday 20th March 1994 when the Ashey Races were re-enacted, and special trains were run to bring people to the event. This was so successful that it is now held annually.

Right: The new Wootton terminus opened in 1986 is seen here in July 2008.

Left: The idyllic setting of Ashey halt on the line to Smallbrook is seen in July 2008.

Calbourne returned to traffic in 1995, but almost immediately *Freshwater* had to be taken out of service requiring a new boiler. It returned to duty in June 1998. In the meantime the 25th anniversary of the move from Newport to Havenstreet was marked on Sunday 28th January 1996, with a reunion of many of those involved in the original event and trains hauled by W24.

Into the 21st Century

In 2002 what became known as 'Griffin's Sidings' were opened on the south-west side of Havenstreet to provide much needed storage. News also came through of a grant approaching half a million pounds from the Heritage Lottery Fund. This was a contribution towards a new carriage and wagon workshop, as well as a ten year programme of restoration projects. The workshops were completed in 2004 when they were officially opened by no less a personage than Her Majesty the Queen, who visited the line on 19th May 2004. This maintained the royal connection started by her Great Grandmother, Queen Victoria.

To bring the story more or less up to date, in 2005, as reported earlier, *Ajax* was put into service. New motive power arrived in February 2005 in the form of another Hunslet Austerity *Waggoner*, which came on loan when the National Army Transport Museum at Beverley closed.

Then in 2006 Ivatt 2-6-2 tank No.41313 arrived, and is currently undergoing restoration having been joined by sister locomotive No.41298. Therefore, it might not be long before one of the options of the 1960s British Railways plan, to use similar tank locomotives on the Island, actually comes to fruition. The first tender locomotive to be seen on Island rails also arrived in November 2008, in the shape of Ivatt 2-6-0 No. 46447, which will be restored for static display. These have been donated to the IWSR by the Ivatt Trust.

In the meantime the carriage restoration programme continues with ex-LBSCR No.2403 having just been taken into the works. 2010 will also see the return to service of *Calbourne* after another major restoration, hopefully followed by W11 *Newport*, which is being fitted with a new boiler. Another new project is for the building of covered storage for the line's historic rolling stock.

So the Isle of Wight Steam Railway enters another new decade with a seemingly rosy future. I wonder what some of those early railway pioneers such as George Young, who poured so much of his personal wealth into building the Ryde & Newport Railway in the first place, would make of it all?

Map of the Isle of Wight Steam Railway

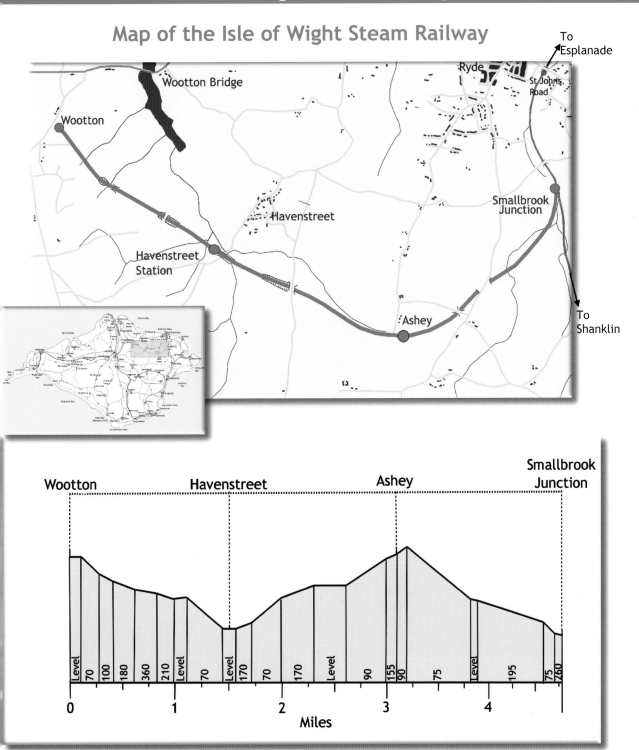

Gradient Map of the Isle of Wight Steam Railway
(Not to scale Gradients in form 1 in x)

Around Havenstreet

Left: The station building at Havenstreet having just been repainted in February 2010 (The station was known as Haven Street until 1958, and both forms of the name are still commonly used).

Right: The former gasworks has been extended and is now the shop and museum, while at the far end there is volunteer accommodation.

Below: Inside the former booking office-cum-signal box at Havenstreet in July 2008.

Right: Ex-LBSCR No.4168, pictured on page 164 being restored in the early days of the society, was again undergoing restoration in July 2008. The underframe of this coach was built in 1905, and with the original body saw service as an ambulance coach during World War One. The current body was built in 1922.

Above: W24 *Calbourne* at the new interchange station at Smallbrook Junction shortly after its opening in 1991.
(Photo: Isle of Wight Steam Railway)

Below: IWSR's *Invincible* exiting Griffin's sidings in October 2007 with a freight train consisting of (from left to right): LSWR Goods Brake Van 56046; LBSCR 10T 5-plank Open 27730; SR 12T 8-plank Open 27936 (rebuilt on underframe of BR open 483701); LBSCR 10T Single Bolsters 59038, 59034, 59050.
(Photo: Alan Doe)

And Finally

Top: An Epitaph. On Christmas Day 1966 Terry Hastings took this picture at Ryde Shed, with no engines in steam and an eerie silence, a foretaste of what was to come. (Photo: Terry Hastings)

Bottom: A future dream. W28 *Ashey* is seen near Fairlee House between Whippingham and Newport on 6th November 1965. Could this scene be re-enacted if the IWSR was ever to achieve the goal of an extension to Newport? I hope so. (Photo: P.F. Bloxam)

Bibliography

A Locomotive History of Railways on the Isle of Wight, D.L. Bradley, RCTS, 1982

A Pictorial Record of Southern Locomotives, J.H. Russell, Foulis-OPC Books, 1991

A Pictorial Guide to Southern Wagons and Vans, T. Gough, Kestrel Railway Books, 2007

An Illustrated History of Southern Wagons Volume Two, G. Bixley, A. Blackburn, R. Chorley & M. King, OPC, 1985

Freshwater, Yarmouth and Newport Railway, A. Blackburn & J. Mackett, Forge Books, 1966,1988

Final Years of Isle of Wight Steam, T. Molyneaux & K. Robertson, Ian Allan, 2007

Island Line, R.C. Humphries, Coach House Publications Ltd, 2003

Isle of Wight Railways Remembered, P. Paye, Oxford Publishing Co., 1984

Isle of Wight Steam Passenger Rolling Stock, R.J. Maycock & M.J.E. Reed, Oakwood Press, 1997

Once Upon a Line, Volumes 1 to 4, A. Britton, Oxford Publishing Co., 1983, 1984, 1990 & 1994

Portrait of the Isle of Wight Railways, H. Kardas, Ian Allan, 1998

Rails in the Isle of Wight, P.C. Allen & A.B. MacLeod, David & Charles, 1967 & 1986

Return to Ryde by Steam, A. Britton, Medina Books, 2005

Ryde By Steam, A. Britton, Medina Books, 2004

South Coast Railways: Ryde to Ventnor, V. Mitchell & K. Smith, Middleton Press, 1985

Steaming Through the Isle of Wight, P. Hay, Middleton Press, 1988

The Bembridge Branch, P.A. Harding, 1988

The Freshwater, Yarmouth and Newport Railway, R.J. Maycock & R. Silsbury, Oakwood Press, 2003

The Great Isle of Wight Train Robbery, R.E. Burroughs, The Railway Invigoration Society, 1968

The Isle of Wight Central Railway, R.J. Maycock & R. Silsbury, Oakwood Press, 2001

The Isle of Wight Railway, R.J. Maycock & R. Silsbury, Oakwood Press, 1999

The Isle of Wight Railway: 40 Years of Preservation, D. Walker & T. Hastings, Nostalgia Road Publications, 2006

The Isle of Wight Railways from 1923 Onwards, R.J. Maycock & R. Silsbury, Oakwood Press, 2006

The Island Terriers, M.J.E. Reed, Kingfisher Railway Productions, 1989

The Piers, Tramways and Railways at Ryde, R.J. Maycock & R. Silsbury, Oakwood Press, 2005

The Signalling of the Isle of Wight Railways, Signalling Record Society, 1993

Various Editions of the *Railway Magazine, Island Rail News* **and** *Southern Railway Magazine.*

Web-Resources

Index of Disused Isle of Wight Stations by Nick Catford on Subterranea Britannica at www.subbrit.org.uk/sb-sites/stations/graphics/wight/iow_station_index.htm

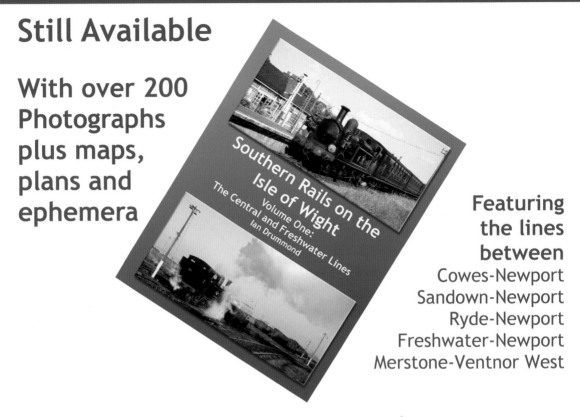